Andrew Preshous   Rachael Roberts
Joanna Preshous   Joanne Gakonga

IELTS Foundation

Teacher's Book Second edition

MACMILLAN

Macmillan Education
Between Towns Road, Oxford OX4 3PP
A division of Macmillan Publishers Limited

Companies and representatives throughout the world

ISBN 978-0-230-42580-4

Text, design and illustration © Macmillan Publishers Limited 2012
Written by Andrew Preshous, Rachael Roberts, Joanna Preshous and Joanne Gakonga

This edition published 2012
First edition published 2004

Designed by Expo Holdings, Malaysia
Illustrated by Oxford Designers and Illustrators Ltd

The authors and publishers are grateful for permission to reprint the following
copyright material:
Page 6: IELTS band descriptors reproduced with permission of Cambridge ESOL;
Page 121: Extract from 'Shopping "is good for your health"' by Billy Kenber © Billy Kenber
2010, first published in *The Telegraph* 14.01.10 reprinted by permission of the publisher.

These materials may contain links for third party websites. We have no control over, and
are not responsible for, the contents of such third party websites. Please use care when
accessing them.

Although we have tried to trace and contact copyright holders before publication, in some
cases this has not been possible. If contacted we will be pleased to rectify any errors or
omissions at the earliest opportunity.

Printed and bound in Thailand

2016 2015 2014 2013 2012
10 9 8 7 6 5 4 3 2 1

Introduction

IELTS is an internationally recognized examination, which is used by organizations all over the world, including universities, employers, and for immigration purposes to assess candidates' English language level.

Demand for IELTS remains high and many students are keen to prepare for IELTS from a relatively early stage in their studies but find it particularly challenging at lower levels. This course takes into account the needs of a learner within the approximate 4–5.5 band range by providing typical IELTS tasks and materials aimed at this level.

IELTS Foundation Second Edition consists of the following components:

- Student's Book
- Class Audio CDs
- Study Skills Book and Audio CD
- Teacher's Book

Coursebook

IELTS Foundation Second Edition is a coursebook that supports the needs of lower level students by offering comprehensive, step-by-step practice within 12 interesting topic-based units. This book takes a systematic approach to preparing overseas students for the Speaking, Listening and Academic Reading and Writing modules of the IELTS exam by providing tips, exam strategies and appropriate practice activities. The suggested time to cover this course is 120 hours, but depending on the level of the students, this could quite easily be shortened or expanded.

The contents are closely based on the IELTS exam assessment criteria and each of the 12 units integrates the four skills thus providing balance and variety. The book also aims to give a thorough grounding in the type of skills necessary to study and perform effectively in an English-speaking academic environment and active learning is encouraged. Therefore, *IELTS Foundation Second Edition* combines two key elements: IELTS preparation and essential study skills.

To complement these elements, relevant grammar sections are also integrated into the units to support the learners in developing the necessary accuracy and range, as well as providing them with useful vocabulary for use in an IELTS and academic context.

There is also a Grammar and vocabulary bank providing additional language practice and model answers with comments for all the writing tasks. For a detailed description of each unit see Contents on pages 8 and 9.

The Teacher's Book

The Teacher's Book provides keys to exercises, including references indicating where answers to reading and listening text questions are to be found, clear teaching notes for every activity in the Student's Book and guidelines and ideas for exploiting the Student's Book material. The Teacher's Book is a very useful guide for those who may be less experienced in this particular area, as it gives comprehensive information about the IELTS exam and the strategies and techniques necessary to achieve a good grade. In addition, it also offers insights into English for Academic Purposes (EAP), particularly the crucial role that study skills play. Audioscripts with highlighted answers are included as well as a number of suggestions for optional activities that can be used to supplement the core materials in the Student's Book. At the back of the Teacher's Book are an extra 12 photocopiable practice activities, each relating to a unit of the book.

Study Skills Book

The Study Skills Book can be used for self-study or as an intensive IELTS preparation course. It is divided into four sections to give further practice in the Speaking, Listening, Academic Reading and Writing modules for the IELTS exam. This workbook includes relevant exercises, sample answers and useful strategies on how to be successful in the IELTS exam. Keys and comments for activities are provided and it also contains a full IELTS practice exam. The Study Skills Book could be used to supplement *IELTS Foundation Second Edition* or as a separate course.

Core skills areas

A summary of the rationale and basic approach taken for each of the core skills areas is provided below:

Reading

Students at this level may find IELTS reading texts too dense to engage with, which prevents them from developing the necessary skills and techniques. The reading material in *IELTS Foundation Second Edition* is designed to be accessible and to have a broad appeal to students from a variety of backgrounds and cultures. Texts have been taken from a variety of sources, including newspaper and magazine articles as well as internet websites.

In each Reading skills section, the student is given guidance in both understanding the text and in learning to deal with the full range of IELTS question types. Skills such as skimming, scanning, prediction, finding topic sentences and guessing the meaning of new vocabulary from context are developed through a series of tasks and students are also given support and useful tips for tackling each type of question. The level of difficulty of the texts increases gradually over the course of the book. Note that in the IELTS exam students will have approximately 20 minutes for each text.

Writing

Many lower level learners do not have the linguistic resources available to produce the kind of answers required in the IELTS Writing module. They may also be unfamiliar with the type of writing expected. These difficulties often result in them producing texts that display an inappropriate style or content, lack organization or contain basic linguistic weaknesses.

IELTS Foundation Second Edition adopts a step-by-step approach that takes lower level learners carefully through each stage of the writing process relating to IELTS Task 1 and 2. Collaborative activities to raise awareness, prepare students and practise key writing skills are provided at each stage. Features focused on include generating ideas, planning, paragraphing, developing an academic style and editing. All units also contain an IELTS Writing question to give individual practice.

As well as focusing on the writing process, a product approach is also adopted by basing tasks on model answers. This gives insights into the type of texts required and the level of language that is desirable. These sample answers also develop students'

ability to evaluate their own work more closely. Relevant language is highlighted and tasks are often complemented by grammar or vocabulary exercises which also help to improve learners' writing. Model answers and comments are provided in the Writing section on pages 160–165 of the Student's Book.

Speaking

IELTS Foundation Second Edition provides guidance and strategies on how to approach the Speaking module. There are numerous opportunities to practise all three parts of the module on a range of topics. Peer and teacher feedback, as well as self-evaluation, are drawn upon to help develop speaking skills. Recordings and audioscripts of student responses are also used for activities and analysis.

To improve students' speaking skills in general, there are regular opportunities to speak in pairs, for example, in pre- and post- reading and listening activities. In addition, language sections throughout the book provide useful words and phrases relating to particular functions such as giving and justifying opinions. Students have the opportunity to prepare and deliver presentations and participate in discussions and debates on interesting and motivating topics. These types of activities will be useful preparation for future academic contexts.

Listening

Many students at lower levels find listening quite challenging, particularly when texts include more academic vocabulary and are extended monologues, such as lectures as in the final part of the IELTS Listening module. Hearing a text only once, as is the case with IELTS, can also cause difficulty. *IELTS Foundation Second Edition* gives students practice in all four parts of the Listening module, as well as providing support and useful tips for tackling different question types.

Audioscripts are provided on pages 166–175 of the Student's Book for easy reference and also in the Teacher's Book, where answers to questions are clearly marked. This book also gives clear guidance on how to develop students' listening skills by focusing on key areas such as prediction.

Language focus

The language focus sections have two major aims: to improve the level of accuracy by focusing on areas which commonly cause difficulty, and to develop the student's range by introducing more variety of expression.

The language work is integrated into the skills work, often highlighted in a reading or listening text. Students are thus encouraged to notice language in context and to try to formulate rules for themselves before going on to use the language in IELTS Speaking or Writing tasks. Further practice of discrete language areas is provided in the Grammar and vocabulary bank on pages 150–159 of the Student's Book.

Vocabulary

The topic-based units help the students to build up key vocabulary around such typical IELTS topics as the environment, health and crime. They are also encouraged to increase the communicative quality of their speaking and writing by learning and using fixed lexical chunks. There is a particular focus on developing knowledge of collocations and building academic vocabulary. Finally, the Grammar and vocabulary bank on pages 150–159 of the Student's Book contains a range of extra activities, focusing on such areas as dependent prepositions and synonyms.

Study skills

Focused exam preparation and practice may not always be enough for students to achieve success at IELTS. At lower levels, a solid grounding in study skills is vital in helping them to develop and improve other areas.

Each of the 12 units in *IELTS Foundation Second Edition* focuses on a particular study skill. The activities provided in these sections will help students develop more effective learning strategies and foster learner independence.

The IELTS Exam

IELTS, or the International English Language Testing System, is an exam designed to assess a learner's level of English, on a scale from 1–9 (see page 6 for details). A summary of each module is outlined below:

Listening

Content: This module is in four sections, which get progressively more difficult, and takes about 40 minutes. The first two sections are based around social situations. Section 1 will be a conversation between two speakers, such as a conversation between a student and their landlord. Section 2 will be a monologue (one speaker) on a subject of general interest, such as a welcoming speech for new members of a sports club. The next two sections are more closely related to education or training contexts. Section 3 will be a conversation between two to four people, such as a seminar in which a group of students discuss a topic. Section 4 will be another monologue, such as a lecture or a talk.

Question Types: There are 40 questions in total, 10 for each section. Different question types include multiple choice, completing notes or sentences, completing or labelling diagrams, charts or tables, classifying and writing short answers.

Exam Tips: Each section is heard ONCE. However, there is time to look briefly at the questions before each part is played. During the exam, students should write on the question paper, and at the end of the exam have 10 minutes to transfer answers to the answer sheet. It is important they do this carefully, and check grammar and spelling, as mistakes will lose marks.

Academic reading

Content: The exam lasts one hour and there are three reading texts, of increasing difficulty, taken from newspapers, magazines, books and journals. The topics are of general interest, so students do not have to be experts in the subject area to understand them.

Question Types: There are 40 questions in total. Question types include multiple choice, *True/False/Not given*, or *Yes/No/Not given*; identifying the view of the writer; completing sentences or notes; completing or labelling diagrams, charts or tables; classifying; matching; choosing paragraph headings, locating information and writing short answers.

Exam Tips: As with the listening module, answers are written on an answer sheet, but no extra time is given for this. It is important for learners to practise managing time so that they complete the whole module within the hour by reading quickly and efficiently.

Academic writing

Content: There are two tasks in this module and it lasts one hour. In Task 1, students are expected to select and summarize the main features in diagrams, charts or tables, and make comparisons using at least 150 words. This might be, for example, a chart showing how young people spend their leisure time. Organization is important and learners need to show that they can clearly present and describe data. Alternatively, students may have to describe the stages of a process, or explain how something works.

In Task 2, an opinion or a problem is stated and students need to write at least 250 words in response to a question related to this. They may be asked to give solutions to the problem, or present arguments in favour and against the opinion, as well as giving and justifying opinions.

Assessment: Assessment is based on whether the question has been answered clearly and appropriately, the organization of the text and the accuracy and range of grammar and vocabulary.

Exam Tips: Learners are advised to spend 20 minutes on Task 1 and 40 minutes on Task 2. It is important to keep to these timings, as Task 2 is longer, and carries more weight than Task 1. It is also important to keep to the word limits, as writing less than the number of words stated is likely to result in a lower score.

Speaking

Content: The Speaking module takes between 11 and 14 minutes and is an oral interview between the student and an examiner, which is recorded. There are three parts to the module. In the first part (4 to 5 minutes), the examiner will ask some general questions about home and family, job or studies, hobbies and so on. In the second part (3 to 4 minutes), the student is given a card with 3 to 4 prompt questions about a particular topic. They have one minute to prepare, when they can write notes if they wish, and will then be asked to speak on the topic for 1 to 2 minutes without any interruption. At the end of this section, the examiner will ask a question. Finally, in the third part (4 to 5 minutes), the examiner will ask some more questions related to the topic in the second part. In this section, they will be looking for the candidate to give opinions and express ideas on more abstract topics.

Assessment: Assessment is based on fluency, the ability to express oneself clearly and naturally without long pauses, the range, variety and accuracy of vocabulary and grammatical structures, and pronunciation.

Exam Tips: It is important that the candidate tries to be as relaxed as possible in the exam. More extended responses to questions, rather than just 'yes' or 'no' answers, will gain higher grades. Students can prepare for this module, for example, by practising speaking for 1 to 2 minutes on different topics. However, discourage students from memorizing long speeches as this type of response is both unnatural and inappropriate.

Further information and strategies on how to approach the IELTS exam are detailed in this book, the Student's Book and the Study Skills Book.

Band 9 – Expert User
Has fully operational command of the language: appropriate, accurate and fluent with complete understanding.

Band 8 – Very Good User
Has fully operational command of the language with only occasional unsystematic inaccuracies and inappropriacies. Misunderstandings may occur in unfamiliar situations. Handles complex detailed argumentation well.

Band 7 – Good User
Has operational command of the language, though with occasional inaccuracies, inappropriacies and misunderstandings in some situations. Generally handles complex language well and understands detailed reasoning.

Band 6 – Competent User
Has generally effective command of the language despite some inaccuracies, inappropriacies and misunderstandings. Can use and understand fairly complex language, particularly in familiar situations.

Band 5 – Modest User
Has partial command of the language, coping with overall meaning in most situations, though is likely to make many mistakes. Should be able to handle basic communication in own field.

Band 4 – Limited User
Basic competence is limited to familiar situations. Has frequent problems in understanding and expression. Is not able to use complex language.

Band 3 – Extremely Limited User
Conveys and understands only general meaning in very familiar situations. Frequent breakdowns in communication can occur.

Band 2 – Intermittent User
No real communication is possible except for the most basic information using isolated words or short formulae in familiar situations and to meet immediate needs. Has great difficulty in understanding spoken and written English.

Band 1 – Non User
Essentially has no ability to use the language beyond possibly a few isolated words.

Band 0 – Did not attempt the test
No assessable information provided.

Contents of the Teacher's Book

Contents of the Student's Book

Content overview

Themes

This unit acts as an introduction to the different parts of the IELTS exam and is thematically focused on the experience of studying overseas.

Exam related activities

Reading

Multiple choice

Writing

Task 1   Data relating to higher education
          Understanding visual information
          Writing an opening paragraph

Listening

Section 1   Form filling
Section 2   Summary completion
             Table completion

Speaking

Part 1   Expanding answers, giving reasons and examples
Part 2   Describing a school subject

Language development

Adjectives ending in -*ing*/-*ed*
Forming questions
Dependent prepositions
Countable/uncountable nouns
Quantifiers

Skills development

Reading

Prediction
Skimming
Matching features

Listening

Predicting answers

Study skills

Identifying parts of speech
Collocations: adjective + noun

Reading   pages 6–8

Aim

This text has been written for students studying in the UK. The level of the language is therefore not as complex as it would be in the IELTS exam. This enables them to start to develop some of the key skills, such as predicting, skimming, matching text with diagrams and choosing the right option in multiple choice, without struggling too much to comprehend the text.

1 Ask students to discuss the questions in pairs or small groups. The discussion should elicit some of the phrases from the next exercise.

2 Students work in pairs to categorize the words and phrases into benefits of living abroad, difficulties of living abroad, or both. Encourage students to give reasons and use their personal experience if they are already living overseas.

Answers

benefits: being independent, meeting new people
difficulties: feeling homesick, feeling lonely, missing friends and family, the language barrier
both: a change in diet, a different climate, experiencing a different lifestyle, experiencing a new culture

3 Predicting content from the title will help students deal with global understanding of the text. Ask students to predict the content of the first part of the text by discussing the meaning of *culture shock*.

4 Encourage students to read the first paragraph quickly to check their predictions. You could set a time limit of two minutes to encourage fast reading.

Answers

experiencing a new culture, meeting new people, being independent, experiencing a different lifestyle, missing friends and family, feeling homesick

5 Ask them to read the first part again to find as many different causes of culture shock as they can.

Answers
- shock of a new environment, meeting lots of new people and learning the ways of a different country
- being separated from the important people in your life: people you would normally talk to at times of uncertainty, people who give you support and guidance
- missing familiar sights, sounds, smells and tastes
- being tired and jet-lagged

6 Ask students to work in groups to discuss what they know about Britain and make predictions about what the author will say about the different points. Students already studying in Britain can talk about any differences they have noticed between these aspects in Britain and their own countries.

7 Ask students to read the text and compare what the author says with their predictions or ideas. Tell them to refer to the glossary if they need help with vocabulary. You could set a time limit for this task of 5 to 6 minutes.

8 In a monolingual group students can compare their own country with Britain. In a multilingual class, encourage students to share information about their own countries and compare with Britain.

Optional activity
Students write about these aspects of culture in their own countries. Alternatively, students could prepare a poster of their countries to present to the rest of the class.

9 This exercise focuses on the adjectives connected to feelings and emotions, which appear in the final part of the text. Ask students to match the adjectives to the definitions.

Answers

1 a	2 e	3 d	4 f	5 g	6 c	7 b

10 Essentially this is a matching paragraphs to headings task, as often found in IELTS, but it also gives students practice in another useful IELTS skill – interpreting diagrams. Look at the diagram together with the class and check that students understand that the stages are in sequence and that the curve represents how positive or negative they are likely to be feeling.

Answers

1 B	2 D	3 E	4 A	5 C

Note that if your students are currently studying abroad, they may well recognize some of these feelings and welcome the opportunity to discuss them.

Multiple choice

Exam information
Multiple choice is a common IELTS task and can be quite challenging, particularly for lower level students. Look at the Strategy on page 8 together.

11 Many students will be familiar with the concept of multiple choice, but encourage them to underline and look for key words (or similar words) and then find the evidence for their choices (or why they have not chosen an option) in the text.

Answers

1 B (paragraph B: ... *you are still protected by the close memory of your home culture.*)
2 A (paragraph E: *Next you may reject the differences you encounter.*)
3 D (encourage students to look at key words: *returning home, advertise, warn*)

12 If your students are still preparing to study abroad, you could use this discussion question to allow them to discuss their plans. If they are currently studying abroad, you could focus the discussion either on what they enjoy about living in this country, or on another country they might like to live in in the future.

Vocabulary   page 9

Adjectives ending in *-ing/-ed*

Aim
This is a common area of confusion for students and the following exercises will be particularly beneficial for improving accuracy when speaking. Ensure that students understand the distinction between the *-ed* and *-ing* adjectives.

1 Look at the example given. Ask students to underline the correct adjective in the other questions and compare their answers.

Answers

1 exciting	3 interesting	5 confused
2 frustrating	4 relaxed	6 fascinating

2 Students discuss the questions from the previous exercise in pairs. Encourage them to give full answers.

3 Look at the example given. Highlight the use of both *-ed* and *-ing* adjectives and encourage the use of both. Students can use a dictionary to check the meaning of any of the adjectives and then have to provide suitable responses to the prompts.

Suggested answers

1 I watched a horror film which was very frightening./I was frightened by a horror film I watched.
2 It was satisfying to finish painting my bedroom./I was satisfied when I finished painting my bedroom.
3 It was exhausting to do a 15 kilometre walk./I was exhausted after doing a 15 kilometre walk.
4 It was surprising that I passed the exam as I expected to fail./I was surprised to pass the exam as I expected to fail.
5 My bus was late, which was annoying./I was annoyed that my bus was late.
6 I saw a young child smoking which was very shocking./I was shocked by seeing a young child smoking.

4 Encourage students to give fuller, more personalized responses here. Monitor and conduct a short feedback slot to elicit a few examples.

Answers

Students' own ideas.

Listening   page 10

IELTS Listening Section 1: Predicting answers

Exam information

This listening is similar in style to Section 1 of the IELTS Listening module, which is the easiest text of the four in the exam, and is a dialogue on a non-academic topic. The context is often students in a social setting, or as in this listening, a student talking to a university staff member about admissions, housing or other non-academic subjects.

Aim

The exercises in this section develop students' prediction skills by encouraging them to guess the type of information required in each question (a number, a name, an address, etc.) and focus on the exam task of form completion.

(O) **1.1** Encourage students to use the information on the form to predict the overall content and the type of answers. Students then listen to complete the form.

Answers

1 Li Cha's personal details and experience of learning English

2 numbers

3 information (nouns)
   Questions 1–10
   1 18
   2 2B
   3 29th October
   4 Hong Kong/China
   5 0825 701 6924
   6 three
   7 playing table tennis
   8 reading
   9 Sydney
   10 computers

Suggestion

Note that in the IELTS Listening module, all recordings are only heard once. However, at the beginning of this course, students might need the security of hearing recordings twice.

(O) **1.1**

[AO = Admissions Officer; LC = Li Cha]

AO: Hello, Li Cha, I'm Susie Shaw, the Admissions Officer.
LC: Hello, pleased to meet you.
AO: I'd just like to talk to you to find out a little more information to give your new tutor, Stephen Ennis.
LC: OK.
AO: How old are you, Li Cha?
LC: I'm eighteen.
AO: OK. Now your start date is next Monday, that's the 14th of February. And you're in class 2B.
LC: Sorry, 2D?
AO: No, 2B. B for Bravo. Do you know when you're finishing? October or November?
LC: I'd like to go home and see my family in November.
AO: Finishing at the end of October then, the 29th. We need a contact number here and one in China, Li Cha. Do you live with your parents?
LC: No, I live with my grandmother and brother, Shao, in Hong Kong. Their telephone number is 8731 4591. And my mobile number here is 0825 701 6924.
AO: Obviously you've studied English before. How long have you been studying?
LC: About three years.
AO: Is that all? You must work hard! I thought you'd been studying for at least five years. Do you have any other hobbies?
LC: Well, I like playing table tennis. I also spend a lot of time emailing friends. Oh, and I like reading. I read in English sometimes too.
AO: Great, that's probably why your English is so good. Now, you want to take IELTS, don't you? Why's that?
LC: Well, I want to go to the University of Sydney. I'd like to study IT and computing.
AO: Really? Would you like to get a job in IT in the future?
LC: Yes, I'd really like to work with computers, there are just so many possibilities.

1 Where do you live?
2 How often do you speak English?
3 What do you do in your free time?
4 Can you speak any other languages?
5 How do you travel to work/school?
6 When did you come to this country?
7 Do you have any brothers or sisters?
8 Can you tell me about your home town?

2 Students then interview their partner using the questions. Encourage them to make a brief note of the answers so that they can report back to the rest of the class.

Expanding answers

Aim
This book aims to develop students' speaking skills with a particular focus on expressing opinions backed up by reasons, and also to help them produce more extended answers. Although activities are primarily in IELTS contexts, the practice given will also help prepare students for seminar and presentation situations at university.

3 Ask students to look at the two short extracts and say which one gives the best answer.

Answer
Student B gives a much more detailed answer.

4 Refer students back to the questions in exercise 1. Ask them to match the four short answers to four of the questions.

Answers

a 1	b 4	c 7	d 6

5 Ask students to match the short answers in exercise 4 with the possible expansions. Feedback as a whole class.

Answers

1 c	2 d	3 a	4 b

Giving reasons and examples

6 This exercise encourages students to add to their answers by giving reasons or examples. Highlight the four different ways of giving reasons and encourage students to give their own reasons for learning English.

7 This exercise again focuses on expanding answers. Ask students to match the sentences to the answers from the previous exercise.

Answers

a 2	b 4	c 1	d 3

Language focus   page 10

Forming questions

Aim
The language focus sections in this book are designed to improve common areas of difficulty. Sometimes students know the rules, but do not apply them in practice. Therefore, many of the activities employ a 'discovery'-type approach, to enable you to assess how much help students need with this area.

1 Go through the form and the first example with the students. Then ask them to write the other questions on a separate piece of paper. Monitor and then correct. Use this opportunity to present question formation including subject/object questions.
Refer students to the Grammar and vocabulary bank on page 150, where there is further practice of question formation.

Answers

1 What's your name?
2 How old are you?
3 Where are you from?
4 How long have you been studying English?
5 What are your hobbies?
6 Why are you taking IELTS?
7 What are your plans for the future?

2 Ask students to work in pairs to ask and answer the questions and complete the form for their partner.

Speaking   pages 10–11

IELTS Speaking Part 1

Exam information
In Part 1 of the IELTS Speaking module, the examiner will ask general questions related to studies, family, future plans and other familiar topics. It is important that students give full rather than brief or monosyllabic answers.

Aim
This section introduces Part 1 of the IELTS Speaking module. It gives opportunities for students to practise forming questions and to find out about each other.

1 The questions in this exercise reflect the type of questions students will be asked in Part 1 of the Speaking exam. Look at the example given. Encourage students to work together to correct the questions.

Practice

Students work in pairs to ask and answer the questions. Encourage expanded responses which include reasons and examples.

Writing   pages 12–13

IELTS Writing Task 1

Exam information

This section introduces IELTS Writing Task 1. In Task 1 candidates often have to describe or present data shown in a diagram. Describing data is also an area that is vital in many academic subjects.

Aim

The exercises in this section familiarize students with different types of visual data and their functions and introduces them to some relevant language.

1 Ask students to discuss the questions in pairs. At this stage discourage them from looking at the charts on the page but to use their own ideas. Get brief feedback as a class.

Understanding visual information

2 It is essential that students can quickly identify the purpose of a diagram and what it is showing. Ask students to look at the four diagrams to check their predictions by matching them to the questions from the previous exercise.

Answers

1 Figure 2	2 Figure 3	3 Figure 4	4 Figure 1

3 Students match the type of chart to each diagram.

Answers

a Figure 2	b Figure 1	c Figure 3	d Figure 4

4 This exercise gets students identifying the main features and significant information shown in this type of diagram. Ask students to select the best alternative from the pairs of words given.

Answers

1 increased	4 less	7 higher
2 fell	5 greater	8 most
3 a quarter	6 under	

5 Students use the information in the four diagrams to complete the sentences using useful words or phrases to describe trends and compare data.

Answers

1 more popular	4 rose	7 just over
2 higher	5 a quarter	8 lower
3 least popular	6 decreased	

The opening paragraph

Aim

It is common for students to copy the wording of the question in their opening sentence. Encourage students not to simply write down the question again but rather try to paraphrase the wording or change it in some way, perhaps by giving a comment about the general trends shown. The extract provides a clear model of a possible opening paragraph.

6 Ask students to look back at the line graph on page 12 and read the rubric provided. They then select the best alternative to complete the model opening paragraph.

Answers

1 shows	3 During	5 trend
2 period/years	4 went up/increased	

7 Ask students to answer the questions by analyzing the model introduction. In feedback it is important to highlight the differences between the rubric and the summary of the general trends shown (as opposed to specific details, which will come in later paragraphs).

Answers

1 present simple
2 no
3 past simple; it describes completed actions in the past
4 general information
5 specific details

Practice

8 This activity will give students the first opportunity to write a short introduction. They can compare what they have written with the models on page 160 of the Writing section.

Speaking   page 14

IELTS Speaking Part 2

Exam information

This section introduces Part 2 of the Speaking module where candidates have to speak uninterrupted for 1 to 2 minutes. Part 2 may be the students' first experience of a longer, uninterrupted turn or mini-presentation. After the student has finished speaking the examiner will ask one or two follow-up questions related to the topic.

1 This is a lead-in and sets the context for the main task. Ask students to discuss subjects they studied at school and their feelings about them. Conduct brief class feedback.

2 After reading the Exam information box in the Student's Book, check that students understand the basic format by asking comprehension questions: *How long do you have to prepare? What is the minimum time you need to speak for? Will the examiner speak in this section?* Ask students to read the exam task on the card quickly and check that they have understood exactly what they have to do. Tell the students they have one minute to make notes on a piece of paper. Students do the task in pairs. Encourage them to check that each of the points on the card has been covered. You could get students to time each other. It is quite possible that at this stage they will not be able to sustain their talk for the 1 to 2 minutes necessary. However, you could ask students to make a note of the time they manage as a motivating target for the next time they practise a Part 2 speaking. Highlight the need to expand answers by giving examples, reasons and details. As whole-class feedback, ask a few students to report back on what their partner's talk was about. This should highlight whether any key points on the card were omitted or if the talk was too short.

3 Students ask and answer the follow-up questions.

Suggestion
Encourage students to:
- use the one-minute preparation time carefully to think about and make a note of what they are going to say
- organize their talk in the order suggested on the card
- keep their talk relevant to the topic and questions on the card
- plenty of practice will ensure they become familiar with this type of task.

Listening   page 14

IELTS Listening Section 2

Exam information
This listening text is a Section 2 text in the Listening module. This is a monologue on a non-academic subject, and is slightly more difficult than Section 1. This kind of text may or may not be in a university context, but it will not be part of a lecture. It will be a talk on a more general subject.

1 Lead into this listening by telling the students that Professor Gooding is going to talk about the difficulties she has had in adjusting to living in different countries and elicit students' ideas about what she liked and the problems they think she might have had in the countries listed. Encourage students to use their

personal experience and knowledge. This discussion should aid understanding when they listen to the talk.

Summary completion

Questions 1–4
 Ask students to read the instructions and check that they have understood. Encourage them to predict what kind of words they are listening for before they hear the text.

Exam information
Note that the instructions state no more than two words or a number for each answer. This is a common IELTS instruction. Ensure students understand that one or two words or a number are acceptable.

Answers

1	International	3 22
2	culture shock	4 fascinated

◎ 1.2

Hello, everyone. Thanks for coming this evening. I've been invited here tonight by the International Students' Society to talk a bit about culture shock. For many of you who have recently arrived from your home countries, life here in New Zealand must seem quite strange and different to you in many ways. Because of my work as an anthropologist, I've had the opportunity to work in quite a number of different countries with quite diverse cultures, so I've had my fair share of culture shock and know exactly how you might be feeling at this time.

Tonight, I want to talk a bit about my own experiences of culture shock and then go on to give you a few hints on how to minimize the effects.

I first left New Zealand when I was only 22 to do some research work on the island of Sumatra in Indonesia. I was interested in learning all about the country and the people, but I was particularly fascinated by the architecture.

In the part where I was working, the buildings have beautiful, curved roofs that I had never seen before and I loved them!

Table completion

Questions 5–10
◎ 1.3 Ask students to look at the table and predict the type of answer before listening. Highlight the numbering in the table so that students can follow easily.

Answers

5 food
6 Egypt
7 short winter days
8 Japan
9 read anything
10 eat with chopsticks

Life in Indonesia is very different from life in New Zealand, and at first I found it very difficult to adjust. The worst thing was looking different to everyone else. I'm about average height in New Zealand, but in Indonesia, I was much taller than most people, and it made me feel very uncomfortable. <u>One of the best things, though, was the food.</u> A change in diet can be one of the biggest problems of moving to a new country, but for me Indonesia was not difficult from that point of view. I'm very keen on spicy food, and there is an Indonesian chicken curry called 'Rendang' that is out of this world!

Climate can be another thing that people find it difficult to adjust to. <u>I found working in Egypt very difficult because of the extreme heat.</u> In contrast, <u>living in Finland was hard because during the winter months the days are so short.</u> Where I was, in the North, it was only light for about four or five hours a day in December. By the end I was pretty good at cross-country skiing, though!

Language is often one of the biggest barriers when you're settling into a new country, but I'm quite good at learning them and this hasn't usually been a problem for me. However, <u>Japan was quite different. I had learned some spoken Japanese before I went</u>, but I hadn't tried to learn to write, so initially, I was a bit nervous about going to a country where <u>I couldn't read anything</u>. This did make life a lot more difficult for me. I couldn't read the destinations on buses, or menus in restaurants, or even road signs.

Sometimes it can be very small things that you're not used to that can make you feel the most homesick. For me, in China, it was connected with eating again. I really love Chinese food, <u>but I found it very difficult to eat with chopsticks.</u> I did learn eventually, but I still prefer a fork! One of the best things about my stay in China, though, was the Professor I was working with at the university. He was really enthusiastic about his work, and that made my job very satisfying.

OK, well enough about my experience. Having mentioned some of the problems I faced, I want to look a bit more generally at how you can adapt to culture shock ...

Dependent prepositions

Aim
Building students' knowledge of dependent prepositions will develop accuracy when speaking and writing.

2 Look at the example and check students understand the idea of dependent prepositions. Then ask them to complete the sentences with dependent prepositions. They can check their answers by listening to the audio again or by looking at the audioscript.

Answers

1	by	3	on	5	about
2	from	4	at	6	about

3 Look at sentences 0 and 5 from exercise 2 and elicit that we use an *-ing* form after a preposition.

4 Students add the missing prepositions to the sentences.

Answers

1	in	3	from	5	about
2	by	4	on	6	about/of

5 Students work in small groups to talk about different countries and cultures. The first person rolls a dice and has to talk about the statement corresponding with the number shown on the dice. Encourage use of adjective/preposition combinations.

Suggestion
It is important that you encourage your students to notice and make a note of verb/adjective/noun + preposition combinations as they read or learn new vocabulary.

Language focus   pages 15–16

Countable/uncountable nouns

Aim
The exercises in the following section will help students develop their accuracy and give practice of a key area of difficulty for students at this level. Further information and practice activities can be found in the Grammar and vocabulary bank on page 150.

1 Check that students understand the basic difference between countable and uncountable nouns. Then ask them to complete the table with words from the box. Monitor and help with any difficulties. In feedback you may need to highlight some of the irregular plurals (*people, children*).

Answers

1 countable: country, language, sports, subjects, university, students, children, people
   uncountable: accommodation, advice, information, weather, luggage, homework
2 singular: country, language, university
   plural: sports, subjects, students, children, people
   NB Uncountable nouns do not have a plural form.

2 Students locate and correct the errors in the sentences.

Answers

1 Ahmed speaks four languages.
2 Accommodation is very expensive in London.
3 The tutor gave me very good advice.
4 The bar chart shows the population of four different countries.
5 correct
6 I went to the library to get some more information about the topic.
7 Team sports such as football and rugby are very popular in this country.
8 When I came to the UK I had a lot of luggage.

Quantifiers

Aim

This kind of language is very frequently used in both Writing Task 1 and Task 2 questions (and indeed in all kinds of academic writing). It is also an area where students often make mistakes. Improving their accuracy in talking about quantity can make a significant difference to the overall accuracy of their writing.

3 Ask students to look at the charts and ask questions about which of these sports they enjoy and find out if their likes/dislikes are similar to the ones in the charts. Then ask them to look at the sentences and go over the example together. Students identify mistakes with quantifiers. You could refer them to the Grammar and vocabulary bank on page 150.

Answers

1 The students spend a lot of time watching football.
2 The majority of the students prefer watching football to playing it.
3 Some of the students like playing basketball.
4 The students don't spend much time playing basketball.
5 The number of students who play table tennis is larger than the number who play football.
6 A large number of students enjoy watching football.
7 Several of the students don't play any sports.
8 Most of the students prefer playing table tennis to watching it.

4 Ask students to write more sentences about the information in the bar charts.

Answers

Students' own answers.

Practice

Aim

This activity gives students the opportunity to carry out a mini class survey and describe the results using some of the language from the unit. This is not only useful practice for IELTS Writing Task 1, but also a good introduction to small-scale academic research.

5 Divide the class into groups and encourage them to choose one of the topics provided (or their own topic, if suitable). They will need to write two or three questions before they carry out the research, eg *What subject would you like to study in the future? Which university would you like to go to?* Monitor this stage to check the accuracy of questions. Students carry out the survey by asking all their classmates and noting down their answers.

6 Ask students to complete a table with their results as shown.

7 Students draw a simple bar chart to show the information they have gathered. Refer students to the two bar charts at the top of page 16 to help them. Students write a short opening statement to describe the findings. They then write sentences to describe the information in the chart. Encourage them to use some of the language from the unit.

8 Ask each group to summarize their findings to the rest of the class. You could highlight on the board any examples of good use of language and/or errors to be corrected (anonymously).

Study skills   page 17

Identifying parts of speech

Aim

A knowledge of parts of speech can help students develop their vocabulary and give them a greater understanding of grammar and sentence structure. When learning any new item of vocabulary, students should be encouraged to identify its part of speech and possible derivatives. Developing this area will help students in all of the four IELTS components.

1 Students read the paragraph from the reading text and identify the parts of speech of the underlined words and find a further example for each group.

Answers

(additional examples in brackets)
a verb – arrive (understand)
a noun – language (accents)
an adjective – embarrassed (regional)
an adverb – quickly (thoroughly)
a preposition – in (than)
an article – the (a)
a conjunction – although (and)
a pronoun – them (they)

2 Highlight the importance of expanding vocabulary by building word families. Students complete the table.

Answers

Noun	Verb
advice	advise
information	inform
arrival	arrive
education	educate
invitation	invite
experience	experience
choice	choose
application	apply

3 Students complete the sentences using words from the box.

Answers

1	experience	5	apply
2	invite	6	education
3	choice	7	advise
4	arrive	8	inform

Refer students to the Grammar and vocabulary bank on page 150, where there is further practice of parts of speech.

Collocations

Aim

One of the key areas of focus in this book is the development of students' awareness and use of collocations (words that commonly appear together). This focus will help expand their vocabulary, be useful for receptive tasks and improve accuracy in productive skills. The *Macmillan Collocations Dictionary* is a useful resource for this area of language.

Adjective-noun collocations

4 Students choose two adjectives for each of the four nouns.

Answers

0 full-time student; undergraduate student
1 higher education; secondary education
2 first language; official language
3 home country; host country

5 Students use one of the collocations from the previous exercise to complete the sentences.

Answers

1 first language
2 host country
3 undergraduate students
4 higher education

2 Earth today

Content overview

Themes

This unit focuses on the environment, looking specifically at global warming, congestion and recycling.

Exam related activities

Reading

Locating information
Yes, No, Not given

Writing

Task 2   Topic sentences
        Introductions and conclusions
        Editing

Listening

Section 3   Short answers
           Sentence completion

Speaking

Part 3   Discussing environmental topics

Language development

Subject-verb agreement
Present simple vs present continuous
The environment

Skills development

Reading

Prediction

Study skills

Working out meaning from context

Lead-in   page 18

1 Look at the photos and elicit some different modes of transport onto the board. Then put students into pairs or small groups and ask them to discuss the problems or benefits of these different modes.

Alternatively you could ask each student to prepare a short (1 to 2 minutes) presentation comparing and contrasting two different modes of transport, which they then present to another student.

2 Ask students to check the meaning of the words and phrases. Depending on the class, you could ask them to work in groups and help each other, or to use dictionaries. Then ask them to divide the words into 'traffic problems' and 'possible solutions.' Checking the answers to this second part of the task will help you to see if all the words have been understood.

Answers

traffic problems: congestion, gridlock, rush hour, traffic jam
possible solutions: bus lane, car pooling, congestion charging, park and ride, road pricing, higher parking charges

3 Ask students to discuss the questions in pairs or small groups. This should provide them with the opportunity to use some of the vocabulary from the previous task.

Reading   pages 18–20

Exam information

The IELTS exam is designed to distinguish between students at very different levels of English. The texts will often be quite complex and contain a lot of unknown vocabulary. Using visual clues and world knowledge to predict the content of the text can help students to follow the main ideas.

Aim

The exercises with the following reading text encourage students to develop the skills of prediction, skimming and scanning, as well as identifying opinions.

4 Ask students to read the title quickly and guess how the text might answer the question.

Then ask students to skim the text quickly, setting a time limit of 2 to 3 minutes, simply to check their predictions.

Aim

One of the major problems students at this level have with IELTS Reading is that they read too slowly and want to look up every word they don't understand. The aim of this exercise is to encourage them to skim for the information they need, rather than trying to process everything. It may help if they just read the first sentence of each paragraph, usually the topic sentence.

Finally, ask them to underline the problems and solutions they can find in the text. This should also help them to gain their first idea of how the text is structured. For example, we can see that Paragraph A is about the congestion charge, Paragraph B about various traffic problems, Paragraph C about road pricing and Paragraph D about parking charges.

Answers

The use of 'actually' suggests that the author is questioning whether it is true.
1 The writer suggests that it is not true.
2 problems: congestion, gridlock, traffic jams
  solutions: congestion charge, road pricing, higher parking charges

Locating information

Aim

To build their IELTS vocabulary, students should be encouraged to notice how much useful lexis there may be within the texts they read that they could also use productively.

5 Ask students to work in pairs. They should try to work out which adjectives and nouns collocate, or go naturally together, before checking their answers by finding the collocating pairs in the text.

Answers

1 c   2 a   3 e   4 b   5 f   6 d

6 Students work individually to consolidate the collocations by writing sentences about their town or city. They could then compare their ideas in pairs. Refer students to the Grammar and vocabulary bank on page 151, where there is further practice of traffic-related collocations.

Locating information

Exam information

Locating information is a common IELTS task. It can be one of the easier tasks, but it is easy to be misled if students simply 'word-spot'. Look at the tip together at the top of page 20.

7 Ask students to read the text again to find which paragraph contains each piece of information. The work they have already done on the vocabulary in the text should help them here.

Suggestion

A useful strategy in the IELTS exam is to highlight or underline the paragraph or section where students found the answer. This is also useful in the feedback slot in order to pinpoint the language used to signify a particular answer.

Answers

1 B   2 E   3 C   4 A

Yes, No, Not given

8 Look at the example given in the tip first and encourage the students to underline the key words in the statement, looking carefully at such phrases as *probably*, *in order to* and *tend to encourage*. Then ask students to check the statements against the views given in the text.

Answers

0 Y (*a tough but necessary decision*)
1 NG (no mention of this)
2 N (London appears to be just as congested)
3 N (it encourages people to drive to out of town shopping centres)
4 Y (*the most obvious reason would seem to be the lack of any real alternative …*)
5 NG (no mention of this)

Language focus   page 20

Singular or plural

Suggestion

Subject-verb agreement is another common area of difficulty where it is relatively easy to improve your students' accuracy. Make sure that they understand the countable/uncountable distinction and that we use a singular verb form with uncountable nouns. Also teach them which form goes with common quantifiers, such as *neither of*.

1 Using the sentences extracted from the text, ask students to identify the subject and the verb forms by underlining them. Then get students to decide if the subject is singular or plural. You can then use this information to show how the verb agrees with the subject.

Answers

subject	verb	singular/plural
1 traffic	has	singular
2 congestion levels	are	plural
3 attempts	have	plural
4 Public transport	is	singular
5 government	needs	singular

2 This section focuses on a number of common errors in subject-verb agreement. Students can work together to identify whether the sentences are correct or not and rewrite the incorrect ones accordingly. Refer students to the Grammar and vocabulary bank on page 151 for further explanation.

Answers

0 Nobody <u>seems</u> to enjoy travelling to work by train. (*nobody* is a singular subject)
1 One of my sisters <u>drives</u> a sports car. (*one sister* is singular)
2 Many of my colleagues <u>share</u> the drive to work. (*many of* is plural)
3 Correct
4 Most people in my country <u>own</u> a car. (*people* takes a verb in the plural)
5 Correct
6 Correct

3 Students should complete the sentences using their own ideas. Monitor to check and elicit a few examples.

Collective nouns, which refer to groups of people, can often take a singular or plural verb form, depending on whether we are thinking of the group as a unit (singular) or a collection of individuals (plural).

Answers

1 is
2 is
3 are
4 has (*have* is also correct as 'government' is a collective noun which can refer to the body or the group of people)
5 is

Refer students to the Grammar and vocabulary bank on page 151, where there is further practice of subject-verb agreement.

IELTS Listening Section 3

Exam information
Although the context of this listening is not strictly academic, it is similar in style to a Part 3 module in the Listening exam. Part 3 is a discussion between up to four people on an academic subject. The context is often students in a seminar or discussing a piece of work.

Aim
The exercises in this section work on two common IELTS tasks: short answer questions and sentence completion.

1 Ask students to work in pairs to describe the pictures, using the vocabulary in the box. Monitor and then check and clarify any unknown vocabulary.

Answers

a recycling bin
b landfill, rubbish, waste
c scrap metal, waste
d bottle bank, recycling bin
A dustbin refers to a large container outside your house where rubbish is stored until it is taken away. Inside the house, a smaller container would be a waste-paper basket, or in the kitchen or bathroom, a pedal bin. Litter is rubbish such as food packaging or waste paper that people have left on the ground in a public place.

2 Ask students to divide the words into two categories. There are at least two different ways of doing this. The task should provide them with an opportunity to consolidate the meaning of the vocabulary.

Possible answers

Managing rubbish responsibly: bottle bank, recycling bin, scrap metal
Not managing rubbish responsibly: dustbin, landfill, litter, rubbish, waste

Things we throw away: litter, rubbish, waste, scrap metal
Places to put waste: bottle bank, recycling bin, dustbin, landfill

Aim
Numbers and figures are an integral part of many academic courses as well as the IELTS exam. Students may well understand the figures, but be unable to pronounce them appropriately or recognize them when heard. This exercise aims to provide practice in a range of ways that numbers and figures may be expressed, and to provide help in this area before the next listening task.

3 (O) **1.4** Ask students to write down the answers using numbers and symbols where possible. They should compare their answers before checking as a class. Clarify any areas of confusion.

Audioscript and answers

⅓
3 million tonnes
59%
54° Celsius
$450
¾
30 kilos
6,900 metres
27th December 2017

4 Ask students how they dispose of their rubbish (including bottles, paper, cans, etc.). Also ask them how they feel if they see people dropping litter and what attitudes people have about this, or what punishments exist for this, in their country.

Short answer questions

Questions 1–6

 Ask students to look at the questions and establish that all the questions are asking for facts and figures. Using the tip, remind students to check the number of words required.

Then ask students to listen and complete the short answer questions.

Answers

1	half a tonne	4	25 million tonnes
2	two-thirds	5	to produce electricity
3	10 per cent	6	by 2020

[L = Lecturer; J = James]

L: ... and today James is going to give us his presentation on household waste disposal. James, are you ready?

J: Yeah, thanks. Well, when I was deciding what to do for this presentation, this topic really attracted me, because it's such an important issue, and it's going to become even more important in the near future when new European law comes into effect. Um ... if you have any questions as I go along, please feel free to ask, and I'll do my best to clarify things.

OK. I think the facts and figures speak for themselves: on average we produce 30 million tonnes of solid household waste <u>every year or around half a tonne per person</u> which is a tremendous amount if you think about it, and obviously it's vital that waste is minimized and disposed of in a way that protects our environment and our health.

We're talking about waste food products, packaging, newspapers, glass, garden waste and so on. In fact, some studies have shown that almost <u>two thirds of our waste is biodegradable</u>; food, paper, natural textiles, for example, and <u>glass, which of course can be recycled, makes up about 10%</u>.

L: Sorry, sorry to interrupt, but can I just ask you if those figures are for the UK only, or are the proportions the same in other countries?

J: No, that's fairly universal, at least in the developed world, but different countries do have very different levels of recycling. In Britain for example, <u>we bury in the region of 25 million tonnes</u> of biodegradable waste; this is known as landfill. I'm sure you can imagine that this is a limited option, particularly in a country with a small amount of land. As well as this, <u>2.5 million tonnes is burned to produce electricity</u>, which is better, but still has environmental problems associated with it, and 2.5 million tonnes is recycled or composted.

L: This is the current situation in the UK?

J: Yes, it is. However, <u>new European law requires us to reduce amounts of waste, and by 2020</u> we will only be able to send 10 million tonnes of this for landfill and the rest will have to be recycled, burned or treated in a different way. So clearly things are going to have to change, and everyone is involved in this issue in some way.

Questions 7–10

 Give students some time to look at questions 7–10. Encourage them to predict the kind of answers that would fit grammatically before listening again, eg 7 must be a verb in the infinitive form.

Answers

7 reduce and reuse
8 glass and paper
9 black rubbish bags
10 past 25 years

[L = Lecturer; J = James]

L: So what exactly is being done?

J: Well, <u>the policy of the government and of environment agencies is firstly to reduce the amount of waste we create to begin with, and secondly, to reuse the waste that is created</u>. Obviously some disposal is necessary but the aim is to limit this as much as possible. What we need to do is to conserve raw materials, like tin and aluminium, while still protecting the environment and public health.

L: Yes, but what does this mean in reality?

J: There are quite a few things that are being done, mostly by <u>local councils. They're responsible for household 'dustbin' collections, or taking away all the rubbish</u> you produce in the home. In recent years, many more sites have been set up to collect waste separately for recycling. There are often containers in car parks or outside supermarkets for people to put <u>bottles in: clear, green and brown bottles are separated. Also newspapers and magazines can be recycled, as well as tins made of aluminium</u>. One of the problems with this, though, is that most people are not bothering to take their rubbish there. To overcome this, <u>some local councils also provide special containers, often called 'recycling bins' for residents to collect glass and paper in</u>. They put these outside their houses at the same time as their rubbish, and they are collected and recycled.

L: I see. So are you saying that recycling is more important than actually reducing waste?

J: No. Nowadays, many products are increasingly being designed with reuse or recycling in mind and I think, in general, people are far more aware about these issues. In some countries, like <u>Switzerland for example, they have put a tax on black rubbish bags</u>, so that people are encouraged not to just throw things straight in the bin, and to reduce their rubbish. Having said that, I think it's still absolutely crucial for the government to continue raising peoples' awareness of the importance of waste management and disposal. <u>Overall, the situation has improved over the past 25 years</u>, and this is mainly because of new laws with tighter controls and higher standards. Even so, individuals and businesses still need to work very hard to reduce and reuse waste as much as possible.

L: Thank you very much. That was a very nice presentation. Does anyone have any further questions?

Sentence completion

5 Ask students to use the verbs in the box to complete the extracts from the recordings. Students have already been exposed to the language; this exercise will help to activate the language so that they can use it productively.

Answers

1 produce, minimized, disposed of, protects
2 reduce, recycled
3 conserve

Language focus   page 22

Present simple vs present continuous

Aim
Many languages do not make a distinction between simple and continuous aspect, which can lead to confusion for students. This exercise looks at the two in context, drawing out the major uses.

1 Ask students to underline examples and compare their answers. This should check that students can recognize the two tenses as well as providing examples in context. Make sure that students do not confuse the *-ing* form with present continuous (ie *responsible for … taking away all the rubbish*).

Answers

J: <u>They're responsible for</u> household 'dustbin' collections, or taking away all the rubbish <u>you produce in the home</u>. In recent years many more sites have been set up to collect waste separately for recycling. <u>There are often containers in car parks</u> or outside supermarkets for people to put bottles in: <u>clear, green and brown bottles are separated. Also newspapers and magazines can be recycled</u> as well as tins made of aluminium. One of the problems of this, though, is that <u>most people are not bothering</u> to take their rubbish there. To overcome this, <u>some local councils also provide</u> special containers, often called 'recycling

bins', for residents to collect glass and paper in. <u>They put these outside their houses</u> at the same time as their rubbish, and <u>they are collected and recycled</u>.

L: I see. <u>So are you saying</u> that recycling is more important than actually reducing waste?

J: No. Nowadays, <u>many products are increasingly being designed</u> with reuse or recycling in mind and <u>I think, in general, people are far more aware about these issues</u>.

2 Students now use the examples they've underlined to illustrate the rules.

Sample answers

Present simple
1 clear, green and brown bottles are separated/They put these outside their houses …/they are collected and recycled (passive).
2 They're responsible/There are often containers in car parks/some local councils also provide/people are far more aware
Present continuous
1 So are you saying …?
2 many products are increasingly being designed (passive)/most people are not bothering to take their rubbish there.

3 As well as understanding the main uses of present simple and continuous, it is important that students are aware of some common 'state' verbs. Ask students to work in pairs to decide which of the verbs in the list are not usually used in continuous tenses.

Answers

state verbs: belong, know, love, realize, seem, smell, want

4 Either discuss the differences between each pair of sentences as a whole class, or in pairs.

Answers

1 a what are you thinking right now
  b what is your opinion
2 a my opinion is that …
  b I am unwell right now
3 a most people own a car
  b my car is not performing well right now

Refer students to the Grammar and vocabulary bank on page 151, where there is further practice of present simple vs present continuous.

5 This exercise gives students the opportunity to try using the two tenses in context. Ask students to complete the text individually before checking their answers together. In feedback, you could ask why they have chosen simple or continuous in each case.

Answers

1	throw away	6	do not realize
2	shows	7	is growing
3	happens	8	are currently sending
4	goes bad	9	are developing
5	know		

6 Ask students to work on the task in pairs. Emphasize that this should be a discussion task.

Once students have finished, you could ask some pairs to report back to the group

Vocabulary   pages 24–25

The environment

Aim

This section aims to develop students' range of vocabulary for talking about climate change, which is quite a common topic in IELTS. It also provides them with ideas to help them with the following writing task.

1 Ask students to identify the topic the words relate to and ask them to check any words they don't know in a dictionary.

Answer

the environment

2 Students read the text to decide on the best title. Point out that it is always a good idea to read a text before starting any gap-fill exercise.

Answer

B

3 In pairs, or as a class, identify the part of speech needed in each gap. Then ask them to work individually to complete the text with the words from exercise 1. Give students an opportunity to respond to the content of the text. Do they think it is possible to stop climate change? Why/why not?

Answers

1 consequences (noun)
2 the planet (noun)
3 climate (noun; used as an adjective)
4 carbon dioxide (noun phrase)
5 greenhouse (noun; used as adjective in compound noun)
6 emissions (noun)
7 essential (adjective)
8 renewable (adjective)
9 wasting (verb)
10 efficiently (adverb)

4 Ask students to think of individual and government actions that could be taken to slow or prevent climate change. This stage is also preparation for the following writing task.

Writing   pages 25–27

IELTS Writing Task 2

Exam information

This section introduces IELTS Writing Task 2 in which the student is expected to write a subjective essay on a general topic supporting any arguments with relevant ideas and examples or evidence. In this unit, the question asks the student 'To what extent do you agree or disagree?'

Aim

Many essays suffer from a lack of coherence. This unit focuses on the overall organization of an essay and organization within each paragraph, looking at topic sentences and supporting information. Students are taken through a model stage by stage, before writing a parallel task.

1 Look at the essay question as a class and underline key words, eg *Individual actions* have *little or no effect* on *climate change*. For this reason, *worthwhile change* can *only* be made at *governmental level*.

Then ask students to discuss how far they agree with the statement.

2 Students read the model answer and identify the writer's opinion and the paragraph which most clearly shows this. Allow students to briefly respond to the content of the essay, by discussing how the writer's opinion compares with their own.

Answers

The writer agrees; paragraph 2 (reference to government intervention)

Topic sentences

3 Check students understand what a topic sentence is, using the definition in the rubric. Then, depending on how confident the students are, either identify topic sentences together as a class, or individually, before checking as a class.

Answers

paragraph 1   In recent years it has become more and more obvious that climate change is real and that it is starting to affect our planet badly.
paragraph 2   Some people argue that the problem is so huge that only international governmental action can have any real impact.

paragraph 3 However, while the government must take a lead on dealing with climate change, we are also all individually responsible for our own carbon footprint.
paragraph 4 In conclusion, I would maintain that to protect our planet, and all our futures, we will need a combination of effective international agreements, strong government policies and changes in individual behaviour.

4 Again, either as a class, or individually, ask students to identify the topic and the main idea in each sentence, using the example to help them. Writing a clear topic sentence for each paragraph will really help your students to write a coherent argument.

Answers

paragraph 2 topic: government action
main idea: government action is necessary because the problem is very large
paragraph 3 topic: responsibility
main idea: we are all individually responsible
paragraph 4 topic: action required to protect the planet
main idea: action at international, government and individual level needed

5 Using the example given, show how the supporting ideas work together with the topic sentence. Ask students to identify the supporting ideas in the other paragraphs and the paragraph without supporting ideas; establish that this is because the conclusion simply has one main idea.

Answers

paragraph 1 risks of continuing to pollute the atmosphere; considering responsibility
paragraph 2 examples of international and national government action
paragraph 3 individual impact on carbon emissions and examples of individual action required
paragraph 4 no supporting information – only one concluding sentence

6 As a class, identify the topic sentence and elicit how the supporting sentences could be added to make a coherent paragraph. Using the Tip, point out that the topic sentence is usually the first sentence of the paragraph. It can, of course, go in other positions, but at this level, students producing their own work should probably stick to beginning a paragraph with a topic sentence.

Answers

1 b   2 c   3 a

7 Ask students to write their own paragraphs using the topic sentence given. Students could look at each other's examples and highlight at least two errors they find.

Optional activity
You could collect (anonymous) examples of errors from the essays and correct them as a class.

Practice

8 Tell students that they are now going to write a similar essay to the one they have just studied. Ask them to look at the new question and to underline the key words, eg *People will never be willing to make the dramatic lifestyle changes needed to control climate change. For this reason, governments must force people to do so.*

Also draw students' attention to the rubric below the statement: *To what extent do you agree or disagree?* Make sure students consider this in relation to the **whole** question, eg how far do they agree that people will never be willing to make dramatic lifestyle changes? **and** how far do they agree that governments must force people to change?

Give reasons for your answer and include any relevant examples from your own experience or knowledge. This is about backing up their statements with supporting information, saying why they think something and giving concrete examples.

9 Look at the explanation of how to write a good introduction. It is important to stress that the essay question should be reworded, as copying it out will not gain any credit. Ask students to choose the best introduction.

Answer

Introduction 2 introduces the topic of climate change and rewords the statement by referring to people being willing to make small changes rather than unwilling to make dramatic ones.
Introduction 1 is not suitable because it goes straight into giving a personal opinion and is also not directly related to the statement.
Introduction 3 is not suitable because it jumps straight to a final conclusion.

10 Ask students to make a list of ways in which they agree or disagree with the statement, and give examples to back up their ideas. This stage could be done in pairs.

11 Continuing to plan the essay, students should then divide their ideas into paragraphs, putting one main idea in each, before writing these paragraphs, using the introduction from exercise 9. Planning in detail like this may not be something that students are used to, but they should be doing a shorter version of this kind of planning, even in the exam.

12 When students have finished their paragraphs, draw their attention to the sentence stems for conclusions in the Useful language box and ask them to write a conclusion.

Editing

13 Remind students to always check their work quickly when they have finished. If appropriate, students could exchange essays and check each other's work here.

It is a good idea for students to keep a checklist of errors that they know they commonly make.

14 Let students read the model answer on page 160. It is not expected that students should be able to produce an essay to this standard themselves, but the model can help them see where their essay could be improved. You could give them the following checklist for comparison:
Is there one main idea in each paragraph?
Are the main ideas well supported with reasons and examples?
Are the paragraphs in a logical order? Can you see the links between each paragraph?
Does the conclusion relate back to the essay statement and to what has been said in the essay?

Optional activity
You could also ask students to underline any vocabulary related to the topic which they can find in the model answer. (climate change, energy use, recycle, rechargeable, impact (of this) on the environment, lower emissions, greenhouse gas emissions, carbon footprint)

Speaking page 28

1 Ask students to brainstorm vocabulary related to each topic. This could be done in small groups, with each group given a different topic area to prepare.

2 (O) **1.7** Students then listen to the short recordings and note any of the vocabulary they listed which comes up.

3 Look at the table together and check students are clear about the difference between an opinion and a reason. Play the recording again and ask students to complete the table. They can then check their answers together.

Answers

Topic	Opinions	Reasons
Should cars be banned in city centres?	yes	they cause congestion, noise and pollution
Why bother recycling?	lazy about recycling	not convenient
What alternative sources of energy are there and which is our best option?	nuclear power is best option	others don't produce enough power

4 Draw students' attention to the Useful language box and make sure that they understand the difference between a personal and impersonal opinion. Let them listen again and note which phrases are used.

Audioscript and answers

 1.7

1 I can't stand the fact that cars are still allowed in many city centres – they cause so much noise and pollution. At rush hour the traffic is always gridlocked. <u>I much prefer</u> city centres that are pedestrianized, where people can walk around with no worries about too much traffic.

2 I guess I'm quite lazy really as I don't bother recycling much except newspapers. I know we should try and reuse our resources if possible, but sometimes it's just not convenient. I do feel a bit guilty about adding to the amount of landfill but <u>I'm convinced that</u> more people would recycle stuff if there were better facilities, and it was generally easier.

3 Well, er, there are quite a lot of alternatives. There's solar power, wind power, even wave power. And, of course, nuclear power. Some people say that nuclear power is too dangerous. But <u>if you ask me</u>, it's our only real option. The others just don't produce enough power, do they?

5 Students choose one of the topics and write five sentences, giving opinions with reasons and using the vocabulary from the unit. This should enable them to recycle language and will act as a preparation for the final stage.

6 Students should talk together about one of the topics. The previous stage will help them, but they should not be reading aloud from their notes.

Study skills page 29

Working out meaning from context

Aim
The texts used for IELTS often contain a large number of words which will be unknown to students at this level. Therefore it is important to help them develop some strategies for working out the possible meaning of a word from its context. This section aims to help them learn how to do this. It is recommended that you carry out similar activities with other texts on a regular basis.

1 Ask students to look at the title of the short article and make predictions. This is a useful habit to encourage in your students whenever they read a text.

2 Students then read the text to check their predictions. It is important that students gain an overall understanding of the text before they start to try to work out the meaning of unknown words.

Answers

Reasons: regeneration of cities where people live close to city centres so require less transport; socializing on the internet

3 Work through the example given as a class and then ask them to complete the five further questions before checking as a class.

Answers

1 decline	4 marked
2 mirrors	5 a factor
3 regeneration	

Extra activity

You could carry out the following similar activity with the text on pages 18–19.
1 business activity, especially the amount of goods or products which are sold (para A – trade)
2 stopped making progress or developing (para C – stalled)
3 the period when the greatest number of people are doing the same thing (para C – peak time)
4 a written request, signed by a lot of people, asking someone in authority to do something or change something (para C – petition)
5 put into action after being officially decided (para D – implemented)
6 control or limit something (para F – curb)
7 the basic systems that a country needs in order to work properly (para F – infrastructure)

Content overview

Themes

This unit is based around the theme of travel and tourism, and includes a number of different destinations, as well as focusing on some more unusual holidays.

Exam related activities

Reading

Matching headings to paragraphs
Short answers

Writing

Task 1 Data describing tourism in different countries
Selecting and reporting the main features
Describing trends and changes over time
Adding specific details to general statements

Listening

Section 1 Table completion
Labelling a diagram
Section 2 Multiple choice
Classification

Speaking

Part 2 Describing a tourist destination
Making notes

Language development

Synonyms
Articles
Describing locations

Skills development

Reading

Skimming
Prediction

Listening

Prediction
Listening for gist

Speaking

Giving a presentation

Study skills

Editing
Collocations: *travel* and *traveller*

Reading   pages 30–32

Aim
The exercises in this section will help students develop skimming and scanning skills, as well as familiarizing them with the exam tasks of matching headings to paragraphs and short answer questions. The skills of skimming and scanning are necessary in academic life and both are tested in the IELTS exam.

1 Start by looking at the photos and eliciting the type of holidays shown. Put the students in pairs to discuss the questions. In feedback you could highlight any relevant vocabulary.

2 Ask students to look at the headline: *Adventure, Risk and Adrenaline Rush – the appeal of extreme tourism*. Get ideas about the overall content of the text and meaning of extreme tourism before asking students to skim read the first paragraph to check their predictions.

Answer
Extreme tourism is participating in activities which are daring or dangerous.

Matching headings to paragraphs

Exam information
This is a very common IELTS task type. Students need to be encouraged to scan each paragraph quickly for information, rather than trying to understand every word. Looking at the first sentence of each paragraph is a good general strategy, as is locating key lexical clues, although students should be made aware of distracters (words or phrases which may lead them to the wrong answer), eg some words from the headings may also appear in a different paragraph from the one that contains the answers.

3 Before doing the IELTS task tell students to quickly skim paragraphs B–G and briefly elicit the type of holiday they would like to go on. Don't go into too much detail at this stage as the following matching task does this. Check that students understand that there are fewer paragraphs than headings. Look at the example and underline any key words in the paragraph that lead to the answer. You could do one more example together if you feel it is necessary. Encourage students to read the text quickly and highlight any lexical clues they find.

Answers

(lexical clues in brackets)
1 iii (*space tourists, have taken to the skies, view the earth*)
2 i (*Antarctica, coldest continent, freezing, icebergs, snow*)
3 v (*Sahara, hot desert, 50°C, sandstorms*)
4 vii (*climbing, 8,850 metres, Everest, high altitude, highest summit*)
5 iv (*Amazon, rainforest*)
6 viii (*ocean depths, tropical reefs, whales, turtles, marine safari, divers*)

Short answers

Exam information
This type of task requires students to scan for specific information from the text. Students need to know that they should use the exact words as they appear and be aware of the word limit. In this particular exercise there is one question for each paragraph, but this may not always be the case. However, the answers will always be located in the same order as the questions.

Questions 7–13
First ask students to read the questions and identify the paragraph where they will find the answer. Do the first one together as an example.

Answers

7 adventure seekers (para A)
8 (intensive) training course (para B)
9 scientists and researchers (para C)
10 sandstorms and scorpions (para D)
11 (high) altitude (para E)
12 indigenous communities (para F)
13 reinforced cage (para G)

Synonyms

Aim
A knowledge of synonyms is very useful for IELTS reading and listening tasks because the text will contain synonyms of key words in the questions, eg in the extreme tourism text *tourist*, *traveller* and *holidaymaker* are used throughout to mean the same thing. Synonyms will also be useful in speaking and writing tasks to vary the language and avoid repetition.

4 Do an example together before getting the students to locate the remaining synonyms.

Answers

1 dangerous, risky, hazardous
2 faraway, far-flung, remote
3 flora and fauna, wildlife, the natural world
4 daring, intrepid (this refers to people rather than actions), adventurous
5 deserted (adj), wilderness (n), uninhabited (adj)

5 Students complete the sentences with synonyms from the previous exercise before comparing with a partner.

Answers

1 daring/intrepid/adventurous
2 flora and fauna/wildlife/the natural world
3 deserted/uninhabited
4 dangerous/risky/hazardous
5 remote (*remote* is the only appropriate word – though *far-flung* and *faraway* are synonyms, they do not collocate with *village*.)

Refer students to the Grammar and vocabulary bank on page 152, where there is further practice of synonyms of the word *trip*.

Language focus   pages 32–33

Articles

Aim
This exercise deals with the basic rules of use for definite, indefinite and zero articles, a complex area of English that many students struggle with.

1 Ask students to match the examples, which are taken from the text, to the rules. Go through the answers with the class, dealing with any difficulties.

Answers

Indefinite articles
1 c (there are many deserted beaches in the world, we are not specifying which one)
2 b (other examples would be: *a week, a mile, a day*)
3 a (this is the first mention of the course, it is mentioned a second time later in the paragraph with the definite article)

Definite article
4 f (further examples: *the best, the longest, the most interesting*)
5 e (there is only one sun (of the Earth), further examples: *the moon, the Prime Minister* (of this country), *the Pope*)
6 g (further examples: *the Amazon, the Mediterranean, the Rockies*)

7 h (we know which windows are being referred to here; the ones in the space hotel)

8 d (the course has already been mentioned earlier in the paragraph)

Zero article

9 j (these nouns would need the definite article if we were being more specific: *the monkeys which are found in the Amazon ...*)

10 k (if we are being more specific we would need to add the definite article: *the money that is spent on space travel ...*)

11 i (there are some notable exceptions which could be highlighted: *the United States, the United Kingdom*, etc.)

2 Students complete the gaps and then check against the text. For further practice, you can create exercises like this with other texts they read.

Answers

1 the most far-flung and (–) inhospitable corners of the earth.

2 the Sahara is the largest hot desert in the world, spanning (–) North Africa from the Red Sea to the Atlantic Ocean.

3 (–) rainfall here is over 2,000 mm a year.

4 ... whose only human residents are (–) scientists and (–) researchers ...

5 (–) travellers to this region will experience (–) 24-hour sunlight and see (–) magnificent icebergs

6 this holiday to (–) South Africa

7 the wonders of the ocean depths including (–) tropical reefs, (–) whales, (–) turtles ...

8 only separated by the bars of a reinforced cage.

3 This tests students' knowledge of articles through a general knowledge quiz. Encourage students to guess if they don't know the answers, but stress that they should try to use the correct article. To motivate them and make the task more competitive you could award points; one mark for getting the answer correct and one mark for getting the article correct.

Answers

1 the Mediterranean

2 the Queen

3 the sun

4 once a month

5 lions and tigers

6 it's the highest mountain in the world

7 Asia

8 the United Kingdom

9 a shark/a variety of shark

10 the Andes

Refer students to the Grammar and vocabulary bank page 151, where there is further practice of articles.

Listening   page 34

IELTS Listening Section 1: Prediction

Suggestion

This is a Part 1 Listening, which introduces the tasks of table completion and labelling a diagram. Ensure students check the format of the table and the order of the questions before listening. Note that the order of the questions always follows the text.

1 Lead in by asking about train journeys and what kind of information it is necessary to know when enquiring about travelling. In pairs or small groups, students prepare possible questions that might be asked of/by a train enquiry person. This will help students when they hear the text.

Example questions

1 What time does the train leave?
  Do I have to change trains?
  How much is a ticket?

2 What day do you want to travel?
  Where are you travelling from?
  Do you want a single or return ticket?

2 Table completion

Before listening to the recording, draw the students' attention to the tip boxes on page 34, and encourage them to predict the kind of information they will be listening for.

Answers

1 a date

2 a type of journey, ie single or return

3 a class, ie first or standard

4 a time

5 a time

6 direct journey or change of train

Questions 1–6

(O) **1.8** Play the recording, repeating if necessary, and get students to complete the table. Allow time for them to check in pairs while you monitor.

Answers

1 Friday March 4th

2 Return

3 Standard

4 12.38

5 9.15

6 Change at Manchester

1.8

[TEP = Tele-enquiry person; S = Student]

TEP: Hello, National Train Enquiry Line. Can I help you?

S: Yes, please. I'd like to find out about times and prices of trains to Edinburgh.

TEP: Fine. And which station will you be travelling from?

S: Birmingham.

TEP: And when would you like to travel?

S: Umm. Friday March the 4th.

TEP: Will that be a Single or Return?

S: Return please.

TEP: Standard or First class?

S: Standard.

TEP: And what time of day would you like to travel?

S: In the morning, please, um, round about 8 o'clock.

TEP: Right, well, there's a train which leaves Birmingham New Street at 8.05 arriving in Edinburgh at 12.38.

S: OK, let me write that down … leaving at five past eight and getting there at … what time?

TEP: 12.38.

S: 12.38. Thanks. Do I have to change trains?

TEP: No, it's direct.

S: And what about the one after that?

TEP: The next one is at 9.15, arriving Edinburgh at 14.35, with a change at Stockport.

S: OK, leaving 9.50, arriving 2.35.

TEP: No, 9.15.

S: Oh. OK. And what about coming back?

TEP: What time would you like to leave?

S: Late afternoon, please.

TEP: Right. There's one at 16.45 which is direct and gets to Birmingham at 20.21, and the one after that leaves at 18.05, arriving at 21.57 including a change at Manchester.

S: Oh, would that be Manchester Oxford Road?

TEP: Erm, no it's Manchester Piccadilly.

Questions 7–10

 1.9 Students listen to the second part of the recording and complete the table.

Answers

7   £33.50
8   7 days
9   Standard Saver
10 No

 1.9

[TEP = Tele-enquiry person; S = Student]

S: Right. And how much is the cheapest ticket?

TEP: Well, it depends. If you can leave after 9am, it's cheaper. There's an Apex Super Saver which you have to book at least 14 days before you want to travel. That costs £33.50.

S: Thirty three … ?

TEP: Fifty.

S: OK. And what happens if I want to leave before 9am?

TEP: If you can book seven days in advance, then you can buy an Apex Peak Saver. That costs £41.30, but if you can't do that, the next cheapest ticket is the Standard Saver which costs £54 return.

S: So it's £41.30 if I book seven days in advance.

TEP: Yes.

S: And £45 if I don't.

TEP: No, it's £54 for the Standard Saver.

S: Oh, OK.

TEP: If you can travel on a different day of the week, then we have the Off Peak Saver at £38.

S: But I can't travel on a Friday for that fare?

TEP: That's right.

S: Fine. Thanks very much for your help.

TEP: You're welcome.

S: Bye.

TEP: Bye.

Labelling a diagram

Exam information

The kind of diagrams that might be found in IELTS exam questions like this are maps, plans (such as this example), a process or a picture of an object to label.

Suggestion

When doing this kind of question, it is important that students verbalize, even silently in their heads, the information in the diagram. You can also help them by exposing them to different types of diagrams and encouraging them to describe them to each other.

Questions 11–14

 1.10 Give students time before listening to describe the plan of the train station in pairs, including the relative positions of the numbered question boxes. Ensure they notice where the speaker is standing.

Answers

11   ticket office
12   platform 15
13   flower shop
14   toilets

 1.10

[IDP = Information desk person; S = Student]

IDP: Hello, can I help you?

S: Yes, I hope so. I've just arrived, and I'm trying to find my way around the train station. Can you tell me where the ticket office is?

IDP: Yes, of course. Look over there, to your right, the ticket office is to the right of the café as you look at it.

S: Oh yes. Thanks. And are those the platforms straight ahead of us?

IDP: Mmmm – which one do you need?

S: I think I need platform 15.

IDP: Yes – platform 15 is in the far corner.

S: Sorry, I can't see it …

IDP: Just there, <u>behind the flower shop</u>.

S: Oh yes. Great – just one more thing – can you tell me where the toilets are?

IDP: Sure – <u>they're over there, on the left, behind the newsagent's</u>.

S: Thanks for all your help.

IDP: No problem.

Writing   pages 35–37

IELTS Writing Task 1

Aim

Some students tend to want to write about every single feature when describing data which often results in a repetitive, inappropriate answer. This section focuses on the skill of selecting and reporting the main features and aims to develop students' ability to describe overall trends and changes over a period of time.

1 This lead-in activity introduces the topic of tourism in Australia. In small groups, students discuss the questions. You could ask them to estimate how many visitors they think go to Australia from their country (and from the UK) and which country sends the most visitors.

2 Students read the Task 1 question before discussing their predictions from exercise 1. Ask a couple more questions to check comprehension, eg *How many tourists from Canada visited in 2006?* (99,000).

Answer

New Zealand

Selecting and reporting the main features

3 Students select the most suitable **general** description of the data. It is important that students identify the overall trend from the data quickly. This can then possibly be used in the introductory statement (see Unit 1).

Answer

Statement 2: the number of visitors increased from 2006–2010. All countries saw an increase except Japan.

4 Students choose three statements which would be suitable to use and three which would not be suitable. This highlights the importance of focusing on key information and the significant features of the data rather than specific details.

Answers

Include 1, 2, 5 as these show the most significant trends. Do not include 3, 4, 6 as these give specific information about given years rather than trends.

5 Students read the model answer and underline specific sentences about each of the countries. Point out or elicit that specific figures are not always mentioned and that descriptions of general trends are acceptable (… *visitors from Japan to Australia dropped dramatically*). Ask for general comments about the sample answer.

Describing trends and changes over time

6 This section uses the model to help the students 'notice' key phrases to describe trends or changes over time. Students underline the verbs in the model answer and then complete the tables and answer the questions.

Answers

1 **go up:** increased, rose, went up
   go down: dropped, fell, halved

2

Up		Down	
Infinitive	Tense: Past simple	Infinitive	Tense: Past simple
go up	went up	drop	dropped
rise	rose	fall	fell
increase	increased	decrease	decreased

Past simple is used, to describe completed past events.

3

Adverbs describing a big change	Adverbs describing a slower, more regular change	Adverbs describing a small change
significantly dramatically considerably	steadily gradually	slightly

These adverbs help the writer describe how big or small the trend is.

7 As a class, look at the two examples. Then get students to write sentences describing the data for other countries.

Possible answers

1 The number of visitors from Canada increased (very) slightly between 2009 and 2010.
   Tourist numbers from Japan dropped significantly from 2008 to 2009.

2 The number of visitors from New Zealand fell slightly from 2006 to 2007.
   Tourist numbers from France rose gradually between 2006 and 2008.

Adding specific details to general statements

Aim
The following exercises highlight the need to support the statements with specific figures from the data.

8 Focus students' attention on the two examples before getting them to use the figures from the table to add further details to the sentences.

Answers
1 about 30,000 to reach 93,000 in 2010
2 631,000 to 335,000

9 Ask students to read the rubric and look at the table before discussing the questions together.

Answers
General trends: an overall increase in visits abroad, with large increases in visits to Egypt, India and Poland and slight decreases in visits to Spain and the USA.
Specific details: figures which support the general trends and show how figures have changed over time

10 Students complete the task in class or for homework. Students can compare their own answer to the model answer on page 161.

Listening   page 38

IELTS Listening Section 2: Listening for gist

Lead in by asking students about school or college trips they have been on.

1 At this early stage in the course, students may still need to hear the listening texts more than once. Look at the questions, play the recording and then compare and check answers.

Answers
1 Paris
2 five days

⊙ 1.11

Hello. Can I just have your attention for a minute? Thank you. My name is Mary Golding, some of you may recognize me – I used to be a teacher here at the college, but I changed jobs last year, and I now work as the Student Officer. OK, well, I'm in today to tell you about a trip that we've got going to er … Paris. Well, this'll be a good chance for those of you who haven't been to France before to have a look at another country, and Paris is very beautiful. We'll be visiting many of the major tourist sites, sampling some French cuisine and you'll all be able to practise

your language skills! This year there are 30 places available, a big increase on last year when only 20 were able to go. At least four members of staff will be travelling too. I think those of you who come will thoroughly enjoy it. The trip is going to be for five days. Originally we planned to leave on Friday the 30th of March but this has been changed and we will now depart on Saturday the 31st of March. We'll be leaving pretty early in the morning, seven o'clock from college, so you'll have to set your alarm clocks, and we'll be going through the Channel Tunnel on the train, so no ferries or coaches for those people who get seasick or travel sick! We aim to leave Paris on Wednesday at about 11 in the morning and should be back by 10pm that night.

2 Multiple choice

Exam information
Students need to be aware that listening texts often contain distracters; information deliberately designed to catch out students who have not fully understood.

Questions 1–5
Tell students to look at all the options first and check any vocabulary, such as *ferry*. Then play the first part of the recording again for students to complete multiple choice answers. After listening, encourage students to check in pairs, discussing why they chose the answers they did, and if they heard any distracting information which would make them eliminate certain answers.

Answers
1 C (possible distraction that she used to be a teacher)
2 C (possible distraction is that last year 20 students went)
3 B (possible distraction that Friday is also mentioned)
4 D (possible distraction *no ferries or coaches*)
5 B (possible distraction is the mention of 11am)

Classification

Exam information
Classification tasks are used in both Listening and Reading tasks. Note that, unlike matching tasks, each option can be used more than once or not at all.

Questions 6–10
 Check students understand that they have to use the letters *F, I* or *P*, and what they stand for.

Answers
6 I   7 I   8 F   9 P   10 I

⊙ 1.12

So, what will we be doing when we get there? If you look at the diagram of Paris that I've given you, you can see that we're going to be staying in a small hotel near the centre of town. It's actually in the area called Montmartre. The accommodation will be shared, so you'll be in a room with one of your friends – you can obviously choose who you'd like to share with. On the first day we're in Paris, we'll be going on a boat trip, up the River Seine and up the Eiffel Tower, the famous monument in the middle of Paris. There should be a good view from up there. <u>Both of these things are included in the cost of the trip</u>, so you won't need to worry about spending extra money. On the second day, we'll be going to Notre Dame, which is a large cathedral with beautiful stained glass windows. <u>There's no admission charge for this</u>, but there are lots of souvenir shops around, so you might need some money for those! There will be lots of time for having a look around on your own, and doing some shopping – I know that some of you are very keen on that! On the third day, our last day in Paris, you'll be free to do whatever you like. You could go to an art gallery, for example the Louvre is a very famous one, where you can see the *Mona Lisa*. <u>You'll have to pay to get in there</u>, but it's not expensive. The biggest problem is that the queue to get in is often very long. The cost of the whole trip is a hundred and twenty pounds, <u>which includes all of the transport</u>, the hotel, and breakfasts. You'll have to buy other food yourself, so you'll need more money for that. It's a really popular trip, we've had real success with it before, I'm sure those of you who come will really enjoy it.

If you'd like to go, can you sign up on this form on the student notice board by Friday? It'll be first come, first served, so do try and sign up as quickly as you can. Thank you very much, I hope to see some of you on the trip.

Speaking   pages 39–40

Aim

This section builds students' vocabulary around the topic of tourist attractions and geographical features and gives them practice in completing Speaking Part 2 tasks. They also have the opportunity to listen to a model answer.

1 Students discuss the pictures using the vocabulary provided. They can use dictionaries to check unknown words.

Suggested answers

The first picture shows a market scene in North Africa: a friendly atmosphere, colourful markets, street cafés, traditional local customs

The second picture shows Pisa in Italy: historic buildings, interesting museums and galleries, lively nightlife, street cafés, traditional local customs

The third picture shows a national park possibly in North America: a peaceful environment, beautiful views, spectacular scenery, unspoilt countryside

IELTS Speaking Part 2

2 Students label the map. Check that students understand the difference between *village, town* and *city* and that they are familiar with the points of the compass. You could do some further work on this vocabulary by talking about local features in your area.

Answers

1 f	2 c	3 e	4 g	5 h	6 b	7 a	8 d

Making notes

3 Focus students' attention on the two Speaking cards. Ask students to read the notes and match them with the appropriate card.

Answer

Task B

4 Play the recording of a student performing the task. Ask students to consider the questions as they listen. Allow time for discussion in pairs before feedback.

Answers

1 yes
2 yes
3 *I'm going to talk about a place I have always wanted to visit.*
4 *The reason I would like to visit Disneyland is …*
5 She could divide her talk into the structure specified in the question, and speak less hesitantly.

🔘 1.13

I'm going to talk about a place I have always wanted to visit, which is Disneyland in Florida in the United States. It's famous all over the world as the place where you can meet all your favourite characters from Disney movies: Mickey Mouse, Snow White, Cinderella. There are many wonderful things to see there like fairytale castles and you can go on exciting rides from your favourite films. I know it's very popular and so I imagine its crowded and busy all year round – I expect you have to wait a long time for some of the rides but I'm sure it would be worth it. I think there is a parade every day where you can see all the famous Disney characters walking and dancing down the streets with music and afterwards you can meet them and have your photo taken with them. The other thing I would like to do there is go shopping so I can buy lots of souvenirs to remember the trip and gifts for my friends and family. The reason I would like to visit Disneyland is it has been a dream of mine since I was very small. I have always loved Disney films and although I am much older now I still love them today. I think Disneyland is somewhere that the whole family can enjoy, whatever your age, and one day I hope to go with my own children.

5 Divide the class into pairs. Give them a minute to make notes and prepare to do Task A. Encourage students to time their partner and give feedback on his/her performance. Monitor and conclude with an error correction slot.

Presentation

Aim

This extends the skills students need to complete IELTS Speaking Task 2 and also helps them prepare for more academic presentations in their future studies.
Students can carry out research by whatever means is available to them. This could be developed into a larger project, depending on time and resources.

Editing

Aim

Proofreading is a vital skill, not only in IELTS, but in academic studies in general. The main focus here is correcting written drafts for both content and language accuracy.

1 Tell students to look at the table and ask some general comprehension questions, eg *Have overseas visits to the UK increased or decreased? (increased) Which is the most common purpose for visiting? (holiday)*

Ask students to read the sample answer and identify the errors of content and language.

Answers

1 General trends: total number of visits increased, not decreased
   Specific details: visiting friends increased to 9,727 not 8,124 (8,124 is the figure for business visits in the row above)
2 correct forms in brackets
   spelling: hollidays (holidays), droped (dropped)
   articles: the UK, a biggest increase (the)
   verb tense: decrease (decreased), rise (rose)
   adverbs describing trends: Para 1: went up significantly NOT slightly; Para 2: slightly NOT dramatically

Always encourage students to edit their own work before the final draft.

Collocations

2 Using a word diagram like this is a useful way to record and learn vocabulary. Encourage students to make similar diagrams of other collocations they come across.

Answers

Adverbs: extensively, independently, overseas, regularly
Adjectives: adventurous, experienced, frequent, keen
Nouns: air, budget, business, rail (these form compound nouns)

Refer students to the Grammar and vocabulary bank on page 152, where there is further practice of these collocations.

Content overview

Themes

This unit focuses on crime and punishment and the effects on modern society.

Exam related activities

Reading

True, False, Not given
Table completion
Classification

Writing

Task 2   Prisons/discipline in schools
         Understanding the question
         Generating main ideas
         Adding supporting information
         Making a plan
         Checking your answer

Listening

Section 2   Note completion
         Multiple choice
Section 3   Table completion
         Matching

Speaking

Part 3   Useful language for discussions
         Punishment and crime prevention

Language development

Crime vocabulary
Defining relative clauses
Present perfect vs past simple

Skills development

Reading

Scanning
Prediction

Listening

Prediction

Study skills

Using a dictionary

Reading   pages 42–45

Aim

The IELTS reading exam can be very challenging for lower level students. This section of the unit contains two texts, which will give students the chance to practise key IELTS tasks including True, False, Not Given, table completion and classification. It also develops prediction, skimming and scanning skills whilst building vocabulary around the topic.

1 Look at the photographs and elicit the activities. Ask students if they think they are legal or not and establish that they are illegal in some countries. Students then discuss the activities listed in pairs or small groups.

Answer

All of the activities are illegal in the UK.

2 This is a prediction task so students should first discuss which of the crimes are most commonly committed in the UK. They then quickly read the text to locate the crimes mentioned and identify which are not in the text. Set a time limit (2 to 3 minutes) for this task to encourage fast reading.

Answers

All of them are mentioned except:
– Carrying a weapon
– Driving through red lights

Exam information

Remind students that for *True* statements they have to locate information that is the same in the text (usually paraphrased). *False* statements will be different or contradict information in the text. *Not given* statements mean that there is no or not enough information in the text.

3 Encourage students to underline key words in the statement and scan the text for the same or similar words or figures.

Answers

1 False (*25% of those polled were not at all worried ...*)
2 False (*... they have almost become legal ...* but they are **not** legal)
3 True (*Over 50%* (of 2000 people) *admitted to breaking the speed limit ...*)
4 Not Given (the crime is mentioned but there is no indication of the percentage of people who commit it)
5 True (*After many years of campaigning, Britain has one of the best road safety records in the world* – the implication here is that in the past there were more road accidents but this number has been reduced)

4 Check that students understand the different punishments mentioned. Students then discuss the questions in small groups before whole class feedback.

5 The second text links to some of the crimes included in the previous one. Ask students to skim read to find which crimes are mentioned. Only allow 3 to 4 minutes for this and discourage detailed reading at this stage.

Answers

Eating while driving
Using a mobile phone while driving

6 Table completion

Questions 1–8

Give students time to study the table and elicit the type of answers that they should be looking for, eg Number 1 is a noun relating to a crime, Numbers 2 and 3 are names, number 4 is a punishment. Give them time to read individually before checking in pairs. In feedback get students to say where they found the answers.

Answers

1 police speed trap	5 blowing his nose
2 Sarah McCaffery	6 three penalty points
3 Kevin Story	7 laughing
4 £30 ticket	8 ticking-off

Classification

Questions 9–13

After reading and checking the instructions, suggest that students underline the names and organizations in the text.

Answers

9 D   10 E   11 B   12 C   13 B

Vocabulary   page 45

Crime and the law

Aim

This task focuses on useful crime vocabulary from the reading text. It is also similar to an IELTS reading summary completion task.

1 Encourage students to predict the word class of the missing words. Allow them to use dictionaries to check meaning and then complete the summary.

Answers

1 guilty	5 appealed	8 prosecution
2 penalty	6 convicted	9 lawyer
3 magistrates	7 justice	10 court
4 solicitor		

Discussion

2/3 Students discuss the questions in small groups. This could lead to a whole class discussion.

Refer students to the Grammar and vocabulary bank on page 153, where there is further practice of crime collocations.

Listening   page 46

Aim

This is a Section 2 IELTS Listening task (a monologue on a general subject) and gives practice of two common IELTS question types: note completion and multiple choice.

IELTS Listening Section 2: Note completion

1 Give students time to discuss the questions and predict the kind of information needed, including word class.

Answers

1 a group of people in an area (neighbourhood) who know each other and will notice anything unusual that might mean something is wrong
2 group of people (1); action (2 and 3); some kind of possession (4); types of crime (5 and 6)
3 noun (1, 4, 6); verb (2, 3, 5)

2 Questions 1–6
(○) 1.14 Point out to students that this task states no more than three words. Play the recording for students to complete the form. Listen a second time if necessary.

It's very nice to see so many of you here tonight. I'm Constable Moore and I'm the Crime Prevention Officer for this area. I'm here tonight to talk about 'Neighbourhood Watch'. Can I ask how many of you have been involved with this before? Oh yes, a few of you – that's good. Well, for the rest of you, Neighbourhood Watch is a scheme set up between the police <u>and local people</u> and I'd like to tell you a bit about how it operates.

Basically, it's just common sense and community spirit. Fifty or a hundred years ago, people tended to live in the area that they grew up in and <u>they didn't move around much</u>, so most people would have known their neighbours. They probably knew each other's habits – what times they came home, who their friends were – that kind of thing, and so it was very obvious if something abnormal was happening. If a stranger was hanging around, or if someone was moving things out of a house, usually someone in the area would see what was happening and <u>would call the police</u>, or take some kind of action. In these days where people move around the country so much, you lose a lot of that <u>community spirit</u>. We don't tend to know our neighbours very well, and we feel a bit embarrassed to get involved.

Imagine this scene. One day, you see a large van outside your neighbour's house and some men carrying things out of the house into the van. Without any knowledge or information about your neighbour, most of us would feel too embarrassed to do anything. Meanwhile, your neighbour's house <u>is being burgled</u> and all of his possessions are being stolen in broad daylight!

Another example is <u>vandalism</u> – people might see someone smashing a telephone box or spraying paint on a wall, but usually they don't want to get involved or call the police.

Answers

1 local people
2 move around much
3 call the police
4 community spirit
5 burgled
6 vandalism

Multiple choice

Questions 7–10

1.15 Read through the questions together and check any vocabulary. Play the recording and repeat if necessary.

Answers

7 B   8 A   9 B   10 C

1.15

These kinds of things happen every day. A Neighbourhood Watch scheme aims to bring back a bit of the 'nosy neighbour' in us all, so that we'll know if we <u>see something suspicious</u>, and feel as if we can contact the police.

How much you do is really flexible. It might be as simple as keeping <u>an eye on a neighbour's home</u> while they are away on holiday, or keeping a look out for suspicious things going on in your road. If you have time, you might want to take a more

active role as a committee member, or volunteer to <u>write, print or distribute newsletters</u>. It's really up to you.

Another major benefit of being in a watch programme is that often insurance companies will lower your <u>premium on your house insurance</u>. Talk to your insurance company to check the details on this, sometimes you have to fit suitable locks on your windows and doors first – but this is a worthwhile thing to do, anyway.

Right – has anyone got any questions ...

Vocabulary   page 47

Aim

Crime and punishment is a popular IELTS topic and this section provides some useful vocabulary.

1 Put students into pairs to complete the table, then check as a class. Make sure students are clear about the differences between robbery, burglary and shoplifting, as these are often confused.

Answers

1 burglary	4 robber
2 shoplifter	5 to vandalize
3 to mug	6 to kill someone deliberately

2 Students use the vocabulary from the table to complete the sentences. Do the first one as an example and highlight that the word may change its form.

Answers

1 Vandals	4 shoplifters
2 burglaries	5 muggings
3 murdering	6 robbed

Language focus   page 47

Defining relative clauses

Aim

This unit examines defining relative clauses (non-defining clauses will be examined in Unit 6). These are frequently used in academic writing and are an area in which students often have problems. The two types of relative clauses are often confused; hence they are dealt with separately.

1 Draw students' attention to the four crime definitions and the relative pronouns. Ask them to complete the definitions with an appropriate pronoun. In feedback establish how we use each one (see Answers below) and that *that* can be also used for things and people instead of who or which. Refer students to the Grammar and vocabulary bank on page 152, for further information and practice.

Answers

1 who (people)	3 which (things)
2 where (places)	4 whose (possession)

2 Students underline the relative clause in each sentence. You may want to do the first as an example.

Answers

1 who attacks people in public places and steals their money and possessions.
2 where criminals are kept as punishment for committing a crime
3 which is paid as a punishment for breaking the law
4 whose lives have been affected by crime

3 Before doing this exercise, it would be useful to go through the rules about when we can omit the relative pronoun (*who, which* or *that*). Write the following sentence on the board:

Burglars usually sell the things that they steal quite quickly.

Elicit the subject of the sentence (*burglars*) and the object (*the things*). Highlight that a relative pronoun is not necessary if it refers to the object of the sentence.

Burglars usually sell the things ~~that~~ they steal quite quickly.

You could provide a few more examples to clarify this point before students do the exercise. Students should work individually to complete the sentences and then check in pairs before class feedback.

Answers

1 that/which/none needed
2 where
3 that/which/none needed
4 that/which/none needed
5 whose
6 who/that

Writing   pages 48–49

IELTS Writing Task 2

Aim

This section provides students with guidance for planning an IELTS Writing Task 2 (advantages and disadvantages – using a balanced approach) from the initial stage of understanding the question and generating ideas, to planning the structure. It also gives a sample answer for students to check and correct.

1 Establish the theme by comparing the pictures of modern and older prisons. This may be a subject of which students do not have much knowledge so you may need to facilitate dicussion.

Answers

Modern: has a private bathroom, no bars, a small window, a desk, a mirror (accept any reasonable answers here)
Traditional: bars, no window, no bathroom, smaller, more basic

2 Pre-teach words such as *barbed wire* and *inmates*. Students work in pairs to decide which of the words and phrases relate to older or more modern prisons.

Answers

Modern: classrooms; ensuite facilities; fewer inmates; gyms; large living blocks; personal computers
Older: high walls with barbed wire; overcrowded, dirty conditions; smaller cells; steel bars on windows

3 The vocabulary exercise should lead neatly into the discussion. Students read the IELTS Writing task.

Key stages

4 Ask students to underline the key words in the question. Establish that the question involves giving a balanced argument with both advantages and disadvantages of modern prisons.

Answers

Key words: modern prisons, designed, learning and communication, larger cells, personal computers, policy, criticized

5 Students categorize the ideas into advantages and disadvantages. Remind students of the importance of getting ideas quickly on the main theme; in the exam they will only have a few minutes to do this.

Answers

Advantages: long-term benefits; the chance to study; make inmates into better citizens; improved facilities and living conditions
Disadvantages: expensive; prisoners have an easy life

6 Explain to students that main ideas always need to be supported by examples and further details. Students match the points to the main ideas from the previous exercise.

1 the chance to study
2 long-term benefits
3 make inmates into better citizens
4 improved facilities and living conditions
5 expensive
6 prisoners have an easy life

7 Having a basic plan will improve the organization of the answer. Tell students that the plan does not have to be detailed; a simple outline showing the content of paragraphs is sufficient. After discussing the three plans, students can read the sample answer and check to see which plan has been used.

Answers

Paragraph plan B has been used and is the most appropriate. The introduction is relevant and advantages and disadvantages are covered in the main body and there is a logical conclusion. The overall structure of Plan A is fine, but the introduction does not really link to the theme of modern prisons and the question does not require the student to provide recommendations. Plan C contains irrelevant information in the introduction and new information in the conclusion and the overall structure seems quite confusing.

8 At this stage students would normally write their answer. However, here a sample is provided to show them how ideas can be incorporated into a balanced answer. Students complete the gaps with the main ideas (advantages and disadvantages) from exercise 5. Then, they underline the supporting information.

Answers

1 a   improved facilities and living conditions
   b   the chance to study
   c   make inmates into better citizens
   d   Prisoners have an easy life
   e   expensive
   f   long-term benefits
2 – modernize the older prisons which were often
       overcrowded and dirty (para 2)
   – using computers in modern classrooms (para 2)
   – less likely to commit crimes (para 3)
   – the chance to work out in the gym or do other
       activities in better accomodation (para 4)
   – a waste of money which could have been spent on
       improving crime prevention (para 4)
   – reduce the level of crime (para 5)

9 The final stage of the writing process is to check the answer. Encourage students to find and correct the six errors.

Answers

Grammar: prisons is (are); help prisoners leading (lead)
Vocabulary: punishing (punishment); safety (safer)
Spelling: benifit (benefit); morden (modern)

Practice

10 You could go through the key stages of planning for this IELTS task (ie understanding the question, generating ideas, making a plan, etc.) and then set the task for homework. There is a model answer on page 161 of the Student's Book.

Listening page 50

IELTS Listening Section 3: Prediction

1 Students work in pairs or small groups to discuss the questions. Note that in Western Europe and the USA, truancy may be much more common than in the students' culture, and that whilst truancy can involve children staying away from school with the knowledge and consent of their parents, it is usually thought of as children doing so without this. Elicit key vocabulary and give definitions for *truancy, truant* and *to play truant*.

Possible answers

– Acceptable reasons: illness, doctor's / dentist's appointment, funeral
– Activities: shopping, sport, visit friends
– Students' own answers.

2 Table completion

Questions 1–7

(O) **1.16** Tell students they are going to listen to a radio programme on the subject of truancy. Before you play the recording, give them one minute to read the instructions and questions, then check the format by asking what they have to do in questions 1–7. You could also ask them to predict answers to one or two of the questions or ask them to say what type of answer is required.

Answers

1 crime   5 unhappy at home
2 life of crime   6 schools
3 the weekend(s)   7 over 12,000
4 heavy fines

🎯 1.16

[P = Presenter; R = David Renshaw; L = Lorna Coates]

P: Today on *Burning Issues* we are going to discuss the issue of school absenteeism or truancy. It's been in the news a lot recently because of the woman from Oxford who was jailed because she didn't make sure her two daughters were going to school regularly. First of all, let me introduce my guests, David Renshaw, a government spokesperson, Lorna Coates from <u>The Crime Reduction Charity</u> and Jennifer Simpson, a mother of three from Oxfordshire. Let me start with you, Mr Renshaw. What is the government doing about truancy?

R: Good morning. Well, obviously, children need to go to school. Truancy damages education, of course, but can also lead children <u>to a life of crime</u>.

P: But aren't the new laws about putting parents in prison rather tough?

R: Well, we have introduced imprisonment in some cases, and some people think this is too hard, but it does seem to work. Even the mother who was jailed said that it was a good thing for her children, because they now realize how important it is to go to school. It's not the only measure we have, though. Something else we are thinking about is <u>'weekend' prison sentences</u>. This means that the parent would only go to prison at the weekends, but could still keep their job in the week. We're also considering <u>heavy fines</u>.

P: OK. Thanks for that. Lorna, maybe you could tell us why you think children play truant.

L: Well, I must say that I think the government isn't looking at the reasons why children play truant – they just want a quick answer, and I don't think it'll be successful. Children miss school for many reasons. For example, they might be <u>unhappy at home</u>, or they might have friends who play truant and encourage them to do the same. Peer pressure like this is very strong in teenagers, particularly. Bullying is another common reason. Children who are bullied at school will often avoid going. I strongly believe that more research needs to be conducted into this problem.

P: That's all very well but can you be more specific?

L: Well, for a start, I don't think punishing the parents will have long-term benefits. Everybody needs to work on this together – parents, children, <u>schools</u>, the government and social services. It shouldn't be just the government sending parents to prison.

R: We are obviously trying to make that happen, but it's very difficult. For example, in the spring, there were <u>over twelve thousand youngsters</u> absent from school, and a lot of these were with their parents. Now, if children are missing school with their parent's consent, then the government needs to take tough measures.

L: Yes, but it's not always as simple as that, is it? What I'm saying is that we need to look at the reasons why this is happening.

Matching

Questions 8–10

🎯 1.17 Draw students' attention to the Exam information box and clarify that they need to identify which three out of the six points are mentioned. It would be useful to underline key words in the statements to focus their listening.

Play the recording and ask students to answer questions 8–10.

Answers

B, C, E

🎯 1.17

[P = Presenter; R = David Renshaw; L = Lorna Coates; J = Jennifer Simpson]

P: Right. Let's look at it from a parent's point of view. Jennifer, you live in Oxford and have three teenage children?

J: That's right.

P: So how do you feel about this issue? Do you think that the parents are responsible for children playing truant?

J: Well I think Lorna's right that it is a very complex issue and <u>I tend to agree that you can't punish the parents for the child's behaviour. If a parent is sent to prison or fined heavily, this isn't going to help us to understand the main reasons why their child is missing school. If the child is unhappy or depressed about something at school, this isn't going to help, is it?</u>

P: A good point, Jennifer. So what would be better?

J: <u>I think the emphasis should always be on the child. You need to find out why he or she is missing school.</u> Then you can make decisions on that information about what to do.

L: Jennifer's right and can I just add that this is the approach that our charity would advocate too.

P: <u>Counselling is another effective option.</u> Wouldn't you agree, Lorna?

L: Well, it's certainly a possibility.

P: Do you have anything else to say, Mr Renshaw?

R: I can assure you that the government is considering all of these points and I should add that nothing is definite yet – we are still at the proposal stage.

P: OK. Thank you all very much for contributing to this discussion. And on tomorrow's programme …

Speaking   page 51

Part 3

Aim

This section focuses on improving students' ability to express and justify opinions and to analyse, discuss and speculate about issues. There are practice activities and language input.

1 Read through the questions with students, checking any difficult vocabulary. Don't worry about answering the questions at this stage as the following exercises prepare students with the language skills to do this in exercise 7.

2 🎯 1.18 Students listen to the recording and identify which three questions are answered. Ask some general questions about the responses given.

Answer

The student answers questions 3, 6, 4 (in that order)

Well, <u>that's a good question</u> ... this has actually happened to me and some of my friends. Last year I left my mobile lying on a desk in a classroom and when I came back after break it was gone. I think what people should do is be very careful about personal security and always keep their valuables in a safe place. <u>Personally I think</u> it is a good idea not to show off expensive items like phones as this may tempt some people to steal them.

[pause]

<u>Yes, I think that's very important</u> that there are strict rules on the road to make sure that motorists drive more carefully. For example in my country the government introduced stricter speed limits about three years ago which was very unpopular at the time. However, even though we have only had the law for a few years the number of accidents on the roads has decreased significantly. <u>I'd say that</u> stricter penalties have also made people think more carefully about the way they drive. Some people say that speed cameras are a good way to stop drivers going too fast but <u>I'm not sure that</u> they are effective.

[pause]

<u>Possibly, but</u> as far as I know the police in my country earn quite a lot compared with other jobs and although their job can be dangerous and difficult <u>I believe</u> that it would be better to put more money into education or healthcare.

3 This section provides useful phrases to use in Part 3 of the speaking test as well as other academic speaking contexts such as seminar discussions. Students choose a heading for each category. Check that students understand *fillers* (expressions used to give the speaker thinking time before answering).

Answers

1 Giving opinions
2 Making a suggestion
3 Agreeing or disagreeing
4 Fillers

4 Students listen again and tick the phrases from exercise 3 that they hear.

Answers

That's a good question.
Personally, I think
Yes, I think that's very important
I'd say that
I'm not sure that
Possibly, but
I believe

5/6 Students use prompts to frame an answer to question 1. Monitor and help them with ideas for this example.

7 Students take it in turns to ask each other the questions. Encourage students to use the phrases and to add supporting details. Monitor and then provide appropriate feedback on the strengths and weaknesses of their responses.

Present perfect vs past simple

Aim

This language section focuses on the different uses of the present perfect and compares it with the past simple, an area that students often find difficult.

1 Refer students back to the listening on page 51 from which these sentences are taken. Ask them to match the extracts with the uses a–d.

Answers

1 c (we don't know when in the past the action occurred)
2 a (specific time in the past mentioned – last year)
3 b (the situation started in the past and continues to the present – for a few years)
4 d (the result in the present is that there are now fewer accidents on the roads)

2 Students complete the sentences using the appropriate form. Monitor and provide support as necessary, particularly with irregular verbs.

Answers

1 have eaten	5	rose
2 didn't exist	6	have escaped
3 has been	7	stole
4 have decreased	8	has had

3 Students decide which alternative is correct in each question and then discuss each question as a whole class, or in pairs.

Answers

1 Has crime increased or decreased
2 did the teachers punish
3 Have you heard

Refer students to the Grammar and vocabulary bank on page 152 for further explanation and practice of the present perfect vs past simple.

Class debate

Aim

This activity draws together some of the themes and skills covered in this unit. Both these topics could be considered controversial so you need to be sensitive about which one you choose.

4 The key to a successful debate is to carefully set up each stage and allow plenty of time for preparation.

1 Decide on the topic and check understanding.

2 Divide the class into groups to argue the question, either for or against.

3 Give students time to generate vocabulary, ideas and relevant supporting reasons and examples and to make a note of these. Encourage students to also think about the opposing argument and how they might challenge this. Also remind students of the useful phrases that they can use. You may also want to focus on other areas such as turn-taking and interrupting politely.

4 It is a good idea for one group to present their argument while the other group listens and takes notes before responding. This stage may need careful management to ensure that the debate runs smoothly and as many students as possible are able to contribute. Ensure that you give feedback on positive elements of the debate (content and language) and highlight any key areas for improvement.

Study skills   page 53

Using a dictionary

Aim

Many students feel reluctant to use a good learner's dictionary, such as the *Macmillan Essential Dictionary*, because of the lack of translation. However, a learner's dictionary will contain a lot more information than most bilingual dictionaries or translators, and will be a huge asset to study.

Ask students what type of dictionary they like to use and what they use it for. Elicit other uses.

1 Ask students to try and work out the meaning of the abbreviations through the matching exercise. Check answers briefly as a class.

Answers

1 c	3 h	5 a	7 i	9 g
2 f	4 b	6 d	8 e	

2 Ask students to look in their dictionaries to find an example of each abbreviation in exercise 1.

3 Elicit other abbreviations they find, and clarify anything students do not understand.

4 Now ask students to look up the words listed and answer the questions. A good learner's dictionary should contain all this information.

Answers

1 transitive
2 on
3 illegal
4 American English
5 thieves
6 Antisocial Behaviour Order
7 aggressive, antisocial, bad
8 informal
9 in prison
10 noun

5 This activity encourages learners to use a dictionary to help improve accuracy by checking for grammatical information. Check that students understand that the error is not necessarily the italicized word (as it may be related to a collocation), but this is the word that they should look up. Do the first one together as an example.

Answers

1 litter (uncountable)
2 robbing (you cannot steal a shop, you steal an item)
3 against the law (wrong preposition)
4 made a statement (collocation)
5 police are needed (takes a plural verb)
6 heavy fines (collocation)

Content overview

Themes

This unit focuses on the world of work, including employability skills, advice on job applications and unemployment rates in different countries.

Exam related activities

Reading

Matching headings to paragraphs
Labelling a diagram

Writing

Task 1   Unemployment/workforce composition and earnings
Comparing and contrasting data
Using linkers

Listening

Section 1   Multiple choice
Labelling a diagram
Section 2   Table completion
Completing a flow chart

Speaking

Part 2   Describing a job you would like to do
Part 3   Discussing different aspects of employment

Language development

Describing skills and qualities
Future forms
Comparatives and superlatives
Suffixes

Skills development

Reading

Skimming

Study skills

Word families
Confusing words: *job, work, career*

Reading   pages 54–56

Aim

This text is aimed at young people who are planning their future studies and careers and offers useful information and guidance about the skills and experience desired by employers. Activities provide practice in skimming, matching headings and labelling a diagram.

1 Draw students' attention to the picture and ask them to suggest what the situation is (an interview) and have a brief discussion about what type of job the man might be applying for. Students work in pairs to discuss the questions and decide on the most and least important qualifications, skills and experience for employers.

2 Ask students what they understand by *employability*. Clarify the definition and the role of the CBI. Ask students to match the skills with the definitions.

Answers

1 e	2 b	3 d	4 c	5 a	6 g	7 f

3 Tell the students they are going to read a text on the topic of work. Read the three possible titles and get students to skim read to choose the most appropriate. Set a time limit of two minutes.

Answer

Title 2 is the most appropriate.

Matching headings

4 **Questions 1–6**
Look at the example together. Remind students that there are more choices than they need and that reading the topic sentence (usually the first sentence) in each paragraph will help them focus on the main idea. Encourage students to mark or highlight the sections where they find the answers.

Answers

1 viii (*strong relationships with universities, links with universities*)
2 ix (*the practical nature of the workplace makes work experience very important*)
3 iv (*small businesses are struggling to make links with universities*)
4 i (*employability skills came out on top, businesses rank employability skills ... at the top of their list*)
5 vi (*Employers are very happy with the IT skills ...,There is also some dissatisfaction ...*)
6 iii (*universities should focus on ..., businesses think universities should focus on ...*)

Labelling a diagram

Questions 7–13

Focus students' attention on the diagrams and elicit what they show and whether words or numbers are missing. Ensure students understand the rubric before reading the text to complete the task. Make it clear that students only need read the final three paragraphs. Read the Tip box together and highlight the importance of using the exact words from the text in the answers. You could also mention that questions follow the order of the text.

Answers

7   Important factors
8   employability skills
9   Positive attitude
10 Business and customer
11 Not satisfied
12 82
13 work experience placements

Vocabulary   page 57

Describing skills and qualities

Aim
This section introduces some useful vocabulary to describe personal skills and qualities in a work context.

1 This is a personalized lead in, which gets students thinking about their own qualities in how they deal with different situations. Students discuss the questions in pairs.

2 Students match the adjectives to the sentences from exercise 1. Clarify definitions and check understanding.

Answers

1	positive	6	methodical
2	motivated	7	diplomatic
3	co-operative	8	conscientious
4	inquisitive	9	enthusiastic
5	resourceful		

3 This task focuses on nouns to describe character, often used in a work context. Students match the nouns to the questions.

Answers

1	a risk-taker	4	a communicator
2	an initiator	5	a quick thinker
3	a planner	6	a relationship builder

Practice

4 Clarify any problem vocabulary in the CVs, eg *First Aid, chess, choir*. Students read the CV extracts and decide which of the adjectives and nouns from exercises 2 and 3 would be applicable for each candidate. They should also suggest possible jobs for each candidate.
In feedback accept any answers if justified.

Possible answers

Ben: motivated, positive, enthusiastic, methodical (chess champion), a risk-taker, an initiator (set up own business and won award)
Eve: positive, enthusiastic, motivated (fund-raising for charity), resourceful, inquisitive (student newspaper), co-operative (choir, acting), a planner, a communicator (languages)
Raj: enthusiastic, co-operative (cricket team, member of orchestra), methodical (musician), motivated, a communicator (speaks 3 languages), a quick thinker, a relationship builder (captain of cricket team)

Listening   page 58

IELTS Listening Section 1

1 Tell students that they are going to listen to a conversation between two students about what they want to do when they graduate. Students read the questions to help focus on the type of information required in each answer.

Answers

1 noun: name of department in company
2 noun: type of job
3 noun phrase: factual information
4 noun: type of person/job
5 figure: date
6 figure: time

2 Multiple choice

Questions 1–6

 Play the recording once and then allow students to check their answers together. If necessary play the recording again, but remind students that this will not be possible in the exam.

Suggestion

In the IELTS exam, you do not lose marks for incorrect answers (you only gain marks for correct ones), so if students don't know the answer, it is always worth trying to eliminate one or two wrong answers, and guessing on a multiple choice question. Remind them never to leave a blank.

Answers

1 B	2 A	3 D	4 A	5 C	6 B

1.19

[S = Sally; J = John]

S: Hi, John, how're you doing?

J: Oh, hi, Sal, not too bad. Just beginning to realize that it won't be long before I have to start looking for a job.

S: But the spring term's only just started!

J: I know, but think how fast the last two terms went – we'll be finished before we know it!

S: I guess you're right. It's a bit scary, isn't it? What are you hoping to do?

J: With my degree in business I'd like to go into marketing but I'll probably end up in sales as there may be more jobs there, so I'm not totally sure at the moment. Oh, that reminds me, there's a careers talk next week which we could go to if you fancy it. Anyway, what about you – any plans yet?

S: Well, I really want to get a job overseas. My sister and her two kids live in Australia. She's a doctor and I'd love to go out there, but before that I'm going to look for a job teaching English somewhere in Asia, possibly in China.

J: Really, that'd be great! I'll come and visit you!

S: Yeah, OK. Apparently there's a big demand for English teachers in China, but I'm a bit worried as I'm not really sure how to go about finding a job or how to sell myself, and to be honest I don't know how useful this type of experience will be for my long-term job prospects in this country.

J: It's difficult, isn't it? So what are you doing next Wednesday? Shall we go to this talk?

S: Who's the speaker then?

J: It's a guy called Adam Lorimer, one of the careers advisors – he once came in and talked to us about writing CVs. I thought he was quite good. He used to work in Human Resources apparently, so he should know what he's talking about.

S: OK. Is that the 16th or the 17th of January? Let me just check. OK, it's the 17th.

J: So what do you think? Shall we go?

S: Maybe – what's he going to talk about?

J: Apparently the talk will cover looking for work and writing applications, including tips on how to impress your potential employers.

S: That sounds perfect, actually. What time does it start?

J: Umm, 7.30pm. Why don't we meet a bit earlier – say half past six and have a drink in the café?

S: And where did you say the talk is exactly?

J: Right. It's in the engineering block in ... C something ... I think ... let me double-check ... yes, C13 which is really easy to find as it's on the ground floor. I'll meet you there.

Labelling a diagram

Questions 7–10

 Students look at the diagram to see how it is organized and to predict how the missing locations might be described. Asking questions, eg *Where is location 7?* will help students orientate themselves before listening.

Answers

7 Modern Languages
8 water fountain
9 a café
10 reception area

1.20

[S = Sally; J = John]

S: I've never been to Engineering. Is it the building opposite the Library?

J: No, that's the History faculty. It's opposite Modern Languages.

S: OK. Is there a small garden in front?

J: That's right, with a water fountain.

S: I know.

J: After you've walked in the main entrance you'll see a café directly in front of you. We could meet there and the room where the talk will take place is next to that.

S: Hold on, so C13, the venue for the talk is straight ahead after I've entered the building?

J: Well, slightly to the left from where you are after you've gone into the foyer area. I think there's a laboratory immediately on your left when you go in. If you have any problems there's a reception area to your right next to a big lecture theatre.

S: Think I've got it. I'll give you a call if I'm running late. Better dash now as I'm meeting Tariq in 10 minutes. I'll see you in the café at 6.30 next Wednesday.

J: OK. See you then.

Language focus   pages 58–59

Future forms

Aim

The many ways of expressing the future can cause much confusion. Students at this level need more guidance in order to give them greater variety and accuracy when talking about the future.

1 Refer students to the listening in the previous section, from which the extracts are taken. Look at the examples with the class and use them to establish that we can talk about the future using more forms than just *will*. Students match the sentences to the uses.

Answers

1 d	2 e	3 a	4 b	5 c

2 Students look at further extracts from the listening and choose the most appropriate future form in each case. They can check answers by listening again or referring to the audioscript on page 169.

Answers

1 I'll probably end up   4 are you doing
2 's   5 's he going to talk
3 I'll come

3 To give practice, students form questions from the prompts. Monitor and check they are using the correct form. Then, students ask and answer the questions in pairs. You could ask students to report back about their partner.

Answers

1 Where are you going after class?
2 What are you going to have/are you having to eat this evening?
3 What are you doing next weekend?
4 When does your course finish?
5 When are you taking/are you going to take the IELTS test?
6 What type of job do you think you'll get in the future?

Refer students to the Grammar and vocabulary bank on page 153 for further information and practice of future forms.

Listening   page 59

IELTS Listening Section 2

1 This is a Section 2 IELTS Listening module text (a monologue on a general subject). Elicit from the students as a class what they think a talk about finding and applying for work might include. Students look at the notes and predict possible answers.

2 Table completion

Questions 1–5

 Point out to students that this task states no more than three words. Play the recording for students to complete the notes. Listen a second time if necessary.

Answers

1 specific areas   4 free
2 useful websites   5 (direct) contact
3 agency

Hello everyone. It's good to see so many of you here. Starting your first full-time job is an important time in your lives and it's vital to make sure you find a job that is suitable for you and that you enjoy.

My talk tonight is going to be divided into two main parts: firstly looking for a job and secondly, writing applications. Another important area is interviews, but they'll be discussed in a separate talk. There'll be time for questions afterwards so if you could wait until then to ask anything, I'd be grateful.

Right – looking for a job. I'm going to focus on four key ways to look for work. The first and probably the most traditional way is newspapers and magazines. These are still good places to find jobs although the internet is probably a more popular method nowadays. National papers are still an excellent source and often run adverts for different types of jobs on different days. Find out which day covers information about the line of work you are interested in for each paper. If you are less flexible about where you want to be, local papers are good sources if you are looking for <u>work in specific areas</u>. Another useful place to look is magazines, in particular specialist industry magazines relating to different sectors such as education or business, for example. Of course, most newspapers and magazines will also have websites, so let's briefly turn to online sources.

The majority of you will use this method and one of the main advantages is that you can search for information very quickly and complete applications online. At the end of the talk I'll give you a <u>list of useful websites</u>, on a handout.

The third place to look for work I want to mention is through a job centre <u>or agency</u>. These are located in most towns and cities and this can be an efficient way to look for work as you're actually letting someone else do some of the job searching for you. Most agencies get a fee from your prospective employer so this service is <u>usually free</u>.

Finally, as many of you know, we organize regular careers fairs here when representatives from major companies provide information about job opportunities. This is a great chance to have <u>direct contact</u> with a range of employers. Check the university website for news of future events.

Labelling a flow chart

Questions 6–10

 Draw students' attention to the Exam information box and tell them to look at the flow chart on page 60 in pairs. They should predict what kind of answers they are listening for. Make sure they notice the order of the questions.

Suggestion

When completing this kind of question, it is important that students understand the organization and layout of the flow chart; where it starts (this may be the top, but may also be the middle in a spider type diagram, or the far left-hand side), and how it progresses. Ask them to notice the numbering, as the questions will always be in the order that they are heard, and this will give them a good idea of how to follow the chart.

6   job description
7   job reference number
8   match
9   covering letter
10 the deadline

 1.22

So, you've found a job that you want to apply for. What next? The first step is usually to contact the company by phone or email and ask for an application form <u>and a job description</u>. Refer to the original job advert and make sure that you mention or <u>include the job reference number</u>. Next, read the job description – do your skills, qualifications and experience make you a suitable candidate? When you complete the application form, whether on paper or online, do it carefully and make sure the information you give is specific to the job and not just general. It's really important to say how <u>your skills and experience match the job requirements</u> and what personal qualities you have that would benefit the employer. Remember this may be your first contact with the employer and first impressions count so if the application form is untidy, incomplete or contains loads of spelling mistakes then it's likely to go straight in the bin! After you've completed the form, most applications will also ask you to <u>include a covering letter</u>. It is important to write a brief, formal letter or email about your interest in the job and your general suitability for this position – don't go into too much detail at this point as the vital information will be on the form. Finally, it's always a good idea to get someone you trust to check the form, maybe a close friend, a tutor or one of your parents. They might spot something that you haven't noticed. If it's all OK, send off the application form so that it reaches the company <u>before the deadline</u>. The main thing to remember is that the perfect job for you is out there – if you don't get the first one, just keep trying. Does anyone have any questions?

Language focus   pages 60–61

Comparatives and superlatives

Aim
This is an area of language where students often make mistakes but is very useful in both IELTS speaking and writing.

1 Ask students to identify the jobs pictured and briefly discuss what skills or qualities they would need for each one. Then refer students to the jobs in the box and ask them to discuss the same points.

Answers

police officer, factory worker, teacher
Accept any valid answers for skills and qualities.

2/3 Elicit students' ideas about their preferred jobs or careers. Encourage them to give reasons for their answers.

Answers
Students' own answers.

4 Depending on your class, you might want to refer students to the Grammar and vocabulary bank on page 153 before doing this section in order to go over the basic rules for forming comparatives and superlatives. Students complete the sentences by forming the comparatives.

Answers

1 fitter   5 friendlier
2 better   6 longer
3 more dangerous   7 more stressful
4 more interesting

5 Students make further sentences using the comparative forms of the adjectives given.

Answers

comparative forms: harder than, more boring than, more important than (Students' own answers.)

6 Students complete the sentences by selecting a job and forming the superlatives.

Answers

1 the most interesting
2 the richest
3 the longest

7 Students make further sentences using the superlative forms of the adjectives given.

Answers

superlative forms: the hardest, the most boring, the most important (Students' own answers.)

Speaking   page 61

IELTS Speaking Part 2

Aim
This gives students the opportunity to speak about a job they would like to do in the future, followed by some more demanding Part 3 questions on the topic of work.

1 Refer students to the task on the card and briefly check what they have to do and how long they have.

2 Focus on the example extracts and highlight the language underlined and used in this task. Choose another job, eg teacher, and elicit some similar examples.

3 Students do the task in pairs and give each other feedback. Monitor as they do the task and make a note of any positive and negative points.

Part 3

4 In order to develop confidence and generate ideas, you could get students to prepare answers (in note form) in pairs before pairing them with a different partner for the actual question and answer session.

Writing   pages 62–63

IELTS Writing Task 1

Aim
This section uses a line graph showing unemployment figures in five European countries to introduce further language for comparing and contrasting data. Students will also use comparative and superlative forms from earlier in the unit and there is further practice comparing data in a pie chart and a bar chart.

1 This lead-in section focuses on the topic of unemployment. Students briefly discuss the questions before class feedback. It would be useful to have some current unemployment rate figures ready to inform students if possible.

2 Remind students that it is vital to read the description and to try and understand what the diagram shows. You could ask simple comprehension questions to check this, eg *What is the graph about? What are the main features?* Students read the model answer and complete with appropriate comparative or superlative forms.

Answers

1	higher	4	smaller	7	the highest
2	lower	5	worse	8	the lowest
3	greater	6	better	9	biggest

3 Elicit the meaning and use of the modifiers *much* and *slightly/a little* and ask students to add them to answers 1 and 2 from the previous exercise.

Answers

1 much higher
2 slightly/a little lower

4 Focus on the sentence shown and get students to answer the three questions.

Answers

1 at the start
2 different
3 it is followed by a comma

5 Ask students to find and underline four other examples of contrast markers in the model answer.

Answers

in contrast, despite, whereas, although

6 Students study the use of the contrast markers and complete the rules. You may like to do the first as an example, highlighting the grammatical structure. If this is an area of difficulty you may want to show some further examples.

Answers

1 although   2 despite   3 whereas   4 In contrast

7 Ask students how to combine the sentences in 1 to check understanding of the exercise. They then do the task individually before checking answers in pairs. Focus closely on accuracy, particularly punctuation.

Answers

1 Prices rose in the first quarter. However, they fell slightly in the second quarter.
2 Sales of laptops have increased dramatically, whereas sales of desktop computers have dropped.
3 The service industry is expanding. In contrast, heavy industry is in decline.
4 Nurses' salaries have gone up slightly in recent years, although they are still below the national average income.
5 Despite student fees increasing in recent years/Despite the increase in student fees in recent years, the number of undergraduates is rising steadily.

8 Discuss the questions as a class. Refer students to the pie chart and bar chart and ask them a few general questions to check understanding of the data. Read the Tip box together to highlight the best approach to this type of task where they have to comment on more than one diagram.

9 Students write the task in class or for homework. There is a model answer for this question on page 161 of the Student's Book.

Suffixes

Aim
An awareness of how different word classes tend to be formed can really help students when guessing the meaning of unknown words from context, particularly if their language background is non Latinate. This exercise focuses on some common noun endings. There are further exercises on word families in the Study Skills section of this unit and on prefixes in the Study Skills section of Unit 10.

1 Ensure that students understand the meaning of *suffix* and elicit a few examples. Students refer to the text on page 55 or use dictionaries to identify the word class and complete the table.

Answers

Nouns	Verbs	Adjectives
organization employability placement relationship	prioritize	economic practical satisfied

2 Encourage students to think of more words with these suffixes to add to the table.

3 As students think of further words in a word family, encourage them to identify the word class. Using dictionaries will help them become independent in their learning.

Possible answers
noun: -ation, -ity, -ment, -er, -or, -ship
verb: -ize, -en
adjective: -ic, -al, -ive, -ied, -ed, -less, -ful

4 This exercise focuses on some of the more general meanings of commonly used suffixes. Ask students to find two words in the box to go with each of the suffixes given.

Answers
1 homeless, jobless   4 instructor, visitor
2 skilful, successful   5 industrialize, specialize
3 driver, employer   6 shorten, widen

5 Students use the newly formed words from exercise 4 to complete the sentences. Make sure students realize that they may have to change the form of the word.

Answers
1 successful, specializes
2 jobless
3 visitors, shorten
4 widened
5 drivers, instructor

Word families

Aim
These activities aim to encourage students to build their receptive and productive vocabulary by raising their awareness of different forms of a root word within a word family.

1 Write the word *employ* on the board and ask students what part of speech it is. Try to elicit other words from this root. Then, refer students to the word-family tree and ask them to complete the family tree for the verb *manage*. Encourage them to use dictionaries to check their answers.

Answers
1 manager   5 mismanaged
2 management   6 manageable
3 mismanagement   7 unmanageable
4 managed

2 Check that students understand how these prefixes change the meaning and see if they know any other words with the same prefix.

Answers
mis-: wrong or badly
un-: not

3 Students choose from the two alternatives. In feedback check differences in meaning.

Answers
1 employable   4 mismanagement
2 management   5 unemployed
3 employers

Confusing words: *job, work, career*

Aim
This section focuses on an area of vocabulary related to the unit's theme that often causes confusion. The activities aim to clarify distinctions between the items by looking at common collocations used with these three words.

4 Students discuss the four questions, using a dictionary to check answers if necessary.

Answers
1 all of them
2 work
3 job, career
4 work

5 Using a dictionary, students complete the common collocations.

Answers

1	career	5	work	9	career
2	work	6	work	10	work
3	job, career	7	job	11	job
4	job, career	8	job	12	job

6 After students have completed this activity, make sure they realize which collocations are possible and which ones are not and why.

Answers

1	job	3	career	5	job
2	work/a job	4	job	6	work

Content overview

Themes

This unit focuses on globalization and global markets.

Exam related activities

Reading

Locating information
True, False, Not given
Sentence completion
Identifying the writer's purpose

Writing

Task 1   Milk production/Sugar beet production
Describing a process
Sequencers

Listening

Section 4   Multiple choice
Table completion

Speaking

Part 2   Describing a successful company
Part 3   Discussing issues relating to globalization
Balancing the argument

Language development

Non-defining relative clauses
Vocabulary: money, buying and selling
The passive

Skills development

Reading

Scanning
Guessing meaning from context

Listening

Signposting

Study skills

Academic writing style

Reading   pages 66–67

Aim

This section introduces students to some of the main concepts of globalization and helps them to develop the skill of reading for gist.

1 You could start by eliciting a definition of globalization, or simply by drawing students' attention to the dictionary definition. Ask students what they think are the good and bad aspects of globalization and elicit a few examples. Then ask students to look at the eight points listed and categorize them as either positive effects, negative effects or both. In feedback get students to justify their answers and give examples.

Answers

Positive: 1, 3, 5, 6
Negative: 2, 4, 7, 8
5 could be both (facilitates 3 but causes pollution)

2 Students work together to match the paragraphs with the headings, with a positive and negative aspect under each one. You could set a time limit for this.

Answers

Global Communications: A (negative), E (positive)
Global Travel and Tourism: B (negative), H (positive)
Global Media: F (positive), G (negative)
Global Business: C (positive), D (negative)

3 Students identify which of the points in exercise 1 are referred to. Having completed the previous activity, they should then be in a position to discuss some of the pros and cons.

Answers

Specific effects from exercise 1 referred to in the text are:
1   para C   5   paras E, H
2   paras B, G   6   paras F, H
3   paras F, H   7   not mentioned in the text
4   not mentioned in the text   8   paras D, G

4 The previous activities should help give students ideas for this discussion. Encourage them to think of both positive and negative effects and give specific examples.

Language focus   pages 67–68

Non-defining relative clauses

1 This first activity aims to build on work done in Unit 4 on defining relative clauses, and to raise awareness of the different functions of defining and non-defining relative clauses. Elicit the answers to the questions from the students and establish that the first sentence is a defining relative clause, as covered in the previous unit, and the second one is a non-defining relative clause, which is used to give extra information.

Answers

1 a   2 b

2 Look at the example as a class and then ask students to work individually to identify the two ideas in each sentence. In a feedback session, show how, rather than repeating the subject, we use a relative pronoun.

Answers

1 Main idea: The big tour operators take most of the profits of holidays in developing countries.
Extra information: The big tour operators own airlines, retail chains, cruise ships, hotels, self-catering accommodation and car rentals.
2 Main idea: The value of world exports is over 19 trillion dollars a year.
Extra information: 19 trillion dollars is 36 million dollars a minute!
3 Main idea: A garment worker in Bangladesh would have to save eight years' wages to buy a computer.
Extra information: Bangladesh is one of the world's poorest countries.
4 Main idea: The local people benefit from jobs using their skills and sale of their crafts.
Extra information: They would otherwise have few employment opportunities.

3 Ask students to work together in pairs or small groups to complete the rules by underlining the correct alternative. Feedback as a class.

Answers

1 can   2 cannot   3 cannot   4 are

4 Look at the example with the class and then ask students to write out the combined sentences. Monitor and feedback as a class. Make sure that students place

the relative clause in the correct place, after the noun to which the relative pronoun refers.

Answers

1 Greater cultural contact has been encouraged by tourism, which has more than doubled over the last 20 years.
2 The banana, which is Britain's most popular fruit, is worth more than $10 billion in world trade.
3 Shima, who lives in Bangladesh, earns £28 for a month's work.

Refer students to the Grammar and vocabulary bank on page 154, where there is further practice of non-defining relative clauses.

Listening   pages 68–69

IELTS Listening Section 4

Aim
This is the first time in the book that the students have been exposed to a Section 4 Listening, ie a monologue on an academic subject (a lecture). This is the most challenging part of the Listening module. The activities in this section focus on IELTS multiple choice and table completion tasks, as well as prediction work to support them in these. There is also a brief introduction to signposting language used in lectures and academic presentations.

1 First, ask students what they know about these organizations. Depending on their background, they may already know quite a lot. Students then check their knowledge by matching the organizations with the definitions.

Answers

1 d   2 f   3 c   4 a   5 b   6 e

2 Ask learners to discuss why certain organizations might be pro- or anti-globalization. This may be quite difficult for them, and something that they may not have thought about before. A lot of support at this stage will help with comprehension of the listening text.

Answers

Pro-globalization: The United Nations, International Monetary Fund, World Trade Organization
Anti-globalization: (some) Trade Unions, Friends of the Earth, International Aid Organizations

3 Questions 1–2 and Questions 3–5
(O)1.23 Reassure students that the Section 4 Listening is the most difficult part of the listening, as they will probably find this challenging. Give them as

much support before the listening as you can, ensuring they are familiar with the vocabulary in the questions and the question types. In keeping with the format of the exam, the listening is broken into two parts to give students time to read the questions for each part.

Answers

1/2 C, D	3 B	4 B	5 C

In the first part of today's lecture I would like to introduce you to the topic of globalization. I will start by considering what globalization is. Secondly, I will explain something of its history. Finally, I intend to look at who the main players in globalization are, both for and against it, and briefly summarize their arguments.

So, let us begin with what may seem an obvious point. What exactly is globalization? A lot of people think it is mainly about economics, or increased global trade. However, it can also be seen as increased cultural and technological exchange between countries. Examples might be McDonald's in Calcutta and Japanese motor technology in Britain. Now let us look a little at the history of globalization. There is no agreed starting point, but it could have been about 100 years ago. Certainly, there was a big expansion in world trade and investment then. This was put back considerably as the capitalist world came up against the First World War and then the Great Depression in 1930.

However, the end of the Second World War set off another great expansion of capitalism in 1948 with the development of multinational companies. These were companies interested in producing and selling in the markets of countries all around the world. Finally, globalization really took off when the Soviet Union collapsed.

It's important not to forget the importance of air travel and the development of international communications. The telephone, the fax and now computers and email have all encouraged the progress of international business.

Questions 6–7 and Questions 8–10

 Questions 6–7 are multiple choice and Questions 8–10 are table completion. Ensure students understand the tasks and have predicted the kind of answer (date, number, etc.) that is required to complete the table.

Answers

6/7 A, D	8 1995	9 187	10 business community

Turning now to the main players involved in globalization, we find that there is a clear division between those who are pro-globalization and those who are anti-.

The main organizations against globalization are the environmental organizations, such as Friends of the Earth and Greenpeace, who put forward the belief that globalization harms the environment.

In general, they blame global corporations for global warming and the depletion of natural resources. The most obvious is oil and gas, but there are others such as tropical rainforests, which are cut down for timber, and the resources of the sea, which may be affected by pollution.

Organizations which represent developing countries, including international aid agencies such as Oxfam, are also against globalization. They are concerned that the global organizations, such as the International Monetary Fund and the World Bank, are not doing enough to help the poor and, indeed, may be adding to their problems. Some are critical of the World Trade Organization. They argue that the WTO is making it difficult for poor countries to protect and build their own industries.

Many companies in rich countries also oppose globalization because they are worried that competition from imports will cost them money. A good example is companies that make clothing and shoes. These are among the few industries in which poor countries can provide effective competition with imports of cheap goods, because wages are so much lower than in America or Europe.

Lastly, some trade unions oppose globalization too. They say it leads to a lowering of wages and conditions of work in the developed and the developing world.

Having looked at some of the anti-globalization arguments, let's now consider those in favour. There are, of course, many organizations in favour of globalization. Perhaps the most important one is the World Trade Organization, or WTO. This was set up in 1995 and has 153 member countries. It administers the rules of international trade agreed to by its member countries. The WTO's rules make it difficult for a country to favour their own industry over imports from other countries.

The WTO argues that the growth of trade between countries increases the wealth of everyone. Trade allows those who can produce goods most cheaply to do so, thus giving everyone the best possible price.

Another pro-globalization organization is the International Monetary Fund or IMF. This was established after World War II in 1946. It aims to promote international cooperation on finance and provide temporary help for countries suffering financial problems. The IMF has 187 member countries.

Finally, the United Nations, which was established after the Second World War, has become a promoter of globalization. It has 193 member states and aims to promote a shared set of values in the areas of labour standards, human rights and environmental practices between the UN and the business community.

So, we've seen that there are powerful arguments and important players both for and against globalization. I'd now like to move on to look at some of the key issues for debate. Let us begin by considering the question of global inequality.

Aim

Understanding the signalling language used to structure formal talks, will help students follow lectures, but will also enable them to structure their own presentations in a way that will make them more easily comprehensible. This exercise aims to encourage familiarization with signals or signposts lecturers may use in organizing a talk, in order to help students follow an argument.

4   Check students understand the concepts of introduction, sequencing and so on by asking for one example of each from the list. As an example, elicit a phrase that might be used in the introduction (*In the first part …*) then point out that *I would like to* is also used in the lecture introduction to signal intent and is followed by *introduce you to the topic of globalization*. Let students work together to categorize

the signposts. Check as a class. Play the recording again for students to check answers. This exercise provides an opportunity for students to consolidate their understanding of the text, as well as the signpost phrases. Explain that these phrases are also useful for productive purposes for their own presentations or any formal speaking, eg in seminars.

Answers

Introduction: 4, 6, 10, 11
Sequencing: 3, 4, 9, 10
Changing topic: 1, 2, 5, 8
Concluding/Summarizing: 3, 7

5 Students listen again to order the phrases.

Answers

4, 6, 9, 11, 10, 2, 1, 3, 5, 7, 8

Optional activity
You might like to get students to do mini-presentations on familiar topics so that they can practise using some of the signpost language.

Reading pages 70–72

1 Ask students to look at the Fairtrade logo and say what it represents and what products it is often found on.

Scanning

2 Tell students they are going to read an article about coffee growers. Allow students to look through the statements and guess what the figures refer to before quickly skimming the text to check. Allow them no more than 5 to 7 minutes for the skimming. Remind them that they do not need to understand everything at this stage.

Answers

8.7 billion	The value of worldwide coffee exports in dollars.
100 million	The total number of people who earn their living from coffee.
50	The number of countries which produce coffee.
5	The amount of money in pence received by the farmer for each coffee sold in the West.
20 million	The number of farmers that earn their living from coffee.
150	The number of times that coffee beans can be sold between leaving the farmer and arriving in the supermarket.

True, False, Not given

3 Questions 1–7
Encourage students to look through the statements first

and check any words they don't understand. Then ask students to read the passage to find the answers and check in pairs before whole-class feedback.

Answers

1 F (para B – The Menzas have stayed loyal to the coffee crop)
2 T (para D)
3 NG
4 NG
5 F (para H: there is no noticeable reduction in the supermarket prices of coffee)
6 F (para K: the co-op cannot get finance to buy the crop)
7 T (para K)

Sentence completion

Questions 8–13
Before students start this exercise, make sure they notice the slightly different rubric, ie that they have to choose one or two words, not three. Then allow them to complete the sentences.

Answers

8	(personal) sacrifices	11	negotiating position
9	noticeable	12	cash
10	crop maintenance	13	fair rates

Identifying the writer's purpose

Question 14
Remind students that for this type of question they need to look at the text as whole, and use information such as the type of language, the layout and so on, and who they think the intended reader is. There is no specific advice given in the text, nor any encouragement to protest, although both these things may be implicit.

Answer

B

Guessing meaning from context

4 Ask students to look through the text again to find the words.

Answers

1	fluctuated	4	vicious circle
2	retailing	5	undermining
3	precarious	6	declining

Money, buying and selling

1 Instead of simply matching words and definitions, you could give half the students words 1–5, and the other half words 6–10. They could check their answers and then teach their words to someone from the other group.

Answers

1 b	3 a	5 d	7 f	9 h
2 e	4 c	6 g	8 j	10 i

Aim

This exercise aims to encourage students to notice useful language they could use productively in a writing text.

2 Ask students to divide the phrases into the two categories.

Answers

Prices going up:
5   gains
6   rise
Prices going down:
1   plummeted
2   the drop
3   fall
4   reduction

Language focus   page 73

The passive

Aim

The passive is used much more commonly in academic English than in general English. Because of the emphasis on process, the passive is commonly used in Task 1 Writing tasks, where a process or how something works, is described. This is covered in detail later in this unit and in Unit 7.

1 Students discuss the questions in pairs before brief class feedback. Try to elicit any facts about the history of coffee or where/how it is produced.

2 Students read the text to check their ideas. After a brief discussion on the content of the facts, ask students if they can identify examples of the passive.

Answers

was (first) brought, to be cultivated, is drunk, has been given, is believed, is grown, is produced, must be roasted, (be) ground, being mixed

3 Check students know how to form the passive (subject + verb *to be* + past participle) by asking them to complete the table.

Answers

Present simple	… is (are) grown, is drunk, is believed, is grown, is produced
Past simple	was (first) brought
Present perfect	has been given
Modal verbs	must be roasted
Infinitive form	to be cultivated
Gerund (-*ing*) form	being mixed

4 Tell students that two of the passive examples include an agent (the 'doer' of the action) and see if students can identify them.

Answers

Coffee was first brought … by traders.
One quarter … is produced by Brazil.

5 Using the two examples from the previous exercise, elicit from the students that we use the passive when we are more interested in the actual action than the agent given. Refer them to the first rule and ask them to find two examples of the other two rules.

Answers

1   Coffee was first brought … by traders.; One quarter … is produced by Brazil.
2   coffee is grown (by farmers); it has been given as a medicine (by doctors)
3   Today coffee is drunk all over the world; it is believed …

6 Students use the passive to rewrite the sentences about tea. Highlight the fact that different forms of the passive are used. Do the first as an example together. Monitor and provide help where necessary. In feedback point out that it is important not to overuse the passive and sometimes the active might be better to avoid awkward structures, eg sentence 5.

Answers

1   It is thought that tea originated in China thousands of years ago.
2   More tea is drunk than any other beverage except water.
3   Tea is usually grown in tropical and sub-tropical climates, although it has also been produced in Britain and northern states of the US.
4   Tea was first imported to Europe by Portuguese traders in the 16th century.
5   Teabags began to be used widely in the middle of the 20th century.
6   Nowadays almost a quarter of the world's tea is produced by China.

Refer students to the Grammar and vocabulary bank on page 154, where there is further practice of the passive when describing a process.

Writing pages 74–75

IELTS Writing Task 1: Describing a process

Aim
As an alternative to describing data, students may have to describe a process in Writing Task 1. This type of text is quite common in academic writing, particularly in science subjects, such as describing a natural process or reporting on a practical experiment. This section will build on the students' increased awareness of the passive voice (covered earlier in the unit) and also review and expand their knowledge of linking words and phrases which should enable them to describe a process more effectively.

1 Lead in by asking students to describe the process shown in the diagram to their partner. Point out that it is important to understand what the diagram shows and whether it is a continuous process or a process with a beginning and an end.

2 Students read the three possible opening sentences and select the most appropriate one. State that a simple, introductory sentence is necessary for this writing task.

Answer
Sentence 3 (more academic, use of passive to focus on the process rather than who does it)

3 Point out that the sentences in this exercise have been taken from a model answer but that they are in the wrong order so students should put them in the correct order by referring to the diagram.

Answers
correct order:
e, b, f, d, a, c

4 Elicit an example of a passive form from the sentences (*is packaged*) and ask them to highlight all the other examples. They should check with their partner and also identify which tense is used and why. You could also review why the passive form is common in this type of text.

Answers
is packaged, is cooled and stored, are delivered, is made, is usually pasteurized, is done, are fed, are milked, is collected, is delivered
present simple passive: it is describing a process that regularly happens

Sequencers

5 Before doing this exercise you could elicit from students what type of words they think might be missing from the gaps in exercise 3. Clarify that sequencers are useful linking words to show the different stages of the process. Students use the words from the box to complete the sentences in exercise 3. Note that some are interchangeable.

Possible answers
a After that/At the following stage
b Next/Then
c Finally
d Then/Next
e First
f At the following stage/After that

6 Ask students to identify the phrase that answers this question and elicit the function of this connecting phrase: to show a reason/purpose. You could also state that it is followed by a verb phrase (*kill bacteria*).

Answers
in order to kill any bacteria

7 Students underline the connectors in the sentences before adding the sentences to the model answer in exercise 3.

Answers
1 as; using a milking machine, as this produces more milk overall ... (stage e)
2 because; ... stored in large, refrigerated containers, because it stays fresher ... (stage b)
3 and therefore; kill any bacteria, and therefore ensure that it is safe ... (stage d)
4 so that; delivered to supermarkets and shops so that they can be sold (stage c)

Practice

8 Clarify what the diagram shows then pre-teach/check the meaning of the verbs in the box or allow the use of dictionaries. In pairs, students select verbs from the box to complete the diagram. After checking answers, they should describe the process of sugar production to their partner. Monitor and encourage the use of the passive voice.

Answers
1 unload	6 add
2 shake, remove	7 filter
3 wash	8 heat, evaporate
4 cut up	9 spin
5 extract	

9 This section provides further writing practice in describing a process, allowing students to use recent linguistic input on the passive, sequencers, connectors and non-defining relative clauses. Although this activity could be done for homework, it might be a good idea to do in class so that students get practice adhering to a specified time limit. Refer students to the strategy as a guideline for approaching this type of task.

Answer

See model answer in the writing section on page 162.

Speaking page 76

Aim

This section helps to familiarize students with the format of Parts 2 and 3 of the IELTS Speaking module by listening to a sample answer. It also gives opportunities for speaking practice.

IELTS Speaking Part 2

1 Remind students of the format of this section of the module. Students listen and identify the topic question and key points on this card.

Answers

1 company
2 company it is
3 it is successful
4 the company advertises
5 a car industry

🎯 2.1

I'm going to talk about <u>a company</u> which is called Honda. It's <u>a Japanese company and they sell a range of vehicles such as small family cars, estates and sports cars. They also produce motorbikes.</u> It's a very good company and is well known all over the world. I'm sure Honda products are common in most countries but I've heard that they are especially popular in Asia and Europe.

<u>There are many reasons why Honda is successful but I think one of the main ones is because it produces a new range of models every year.</u> I expect the company has teams of skilled professionals who design and create cars using modern technology, which means new models have many of the latest features. Another reason for Honda's success is that the models are often more economical than some of their competitors – in both price and petrol consumption. Honda also makes expensive luxury cars too and some of these are designed to be very fast. This shows that Honda products appeal to a wide range of people. The company is also successful because parts for these cars are usually very cheap and easy to get in most countries.

<u>As far as I know, Honda advertises new cars on TV quite a lot and these advertisements often look quite stylish. I've also seen their</u>

<u>products advertised in newspapers and on large billboards by the side of the road.</u>
In my country you see many Hondas on the road but these have been imported from overseas as <u>we don't really have much of a car industry.</u>

2 Play the extract again to elicit general comments about the candidate's performance.

Answers

It covers all the main points on the card in appropriate depth, is fluent, accurate and about the right length. A strong answer. See audioscript above for details.

3 Having heard a model answer, students now practise their own versions. Give students one minute to make notes, then they do this task with their partner. Monitor and give feedback.

IELTS Speaking Part 3

4 The Part 3 questions are broadly related to the theme of globalization and this section provides relevant speaking practice. Some preparation time could be given, students then answer questions in pairs before whole-class feedback. You could even set up this section as a group discussion or simulated 'seminar'. Alternatively, at this stage just ask students to read the sample questions; they will get an opportunity to practise at the end of this section.

Balancing the argument

5 🎯 **2.2** Tell students to listen to the recording and identify which question from exercise 4 is being answered.

Answer

The speaker is answering question 5.

6 Play the extract again and elicit answers to the questions. Establish that it is vital to give reasons, not just short or one-word answers.

Answers

1 Cheaper flights mean that more people can afford to travel. More people can experience different cultures and places.
2 More flights cause more pollution. Some tourist destinations have too many tourists and not enough clean water supplies.

🎯 2.2

Well, there are clearly different ways of looking at it. <u>Cheaper flights mean that more people can afford to travel.</u> This has to be a good thing in that <u>more people can experience different cultures and places.</u> On the other hand, <u>more flights cause more</u>

pollution and some tourist destinations have too many tourists and not enough clean water supplies, and so on. As far as I'm concerned though, the benefits outweigh the disadvantages.

7 Draw students' attention to the audioscript on page 171 of the Student's Book so that they can answer the questions. In the final part of this section refer students to the useful language that will give them a little 'thinking' time before they answer the questions. Encourage them to use these phrases as they practise the Part 3 questions from exercise 4.

Answers
1 there are clearly different ways of looking at it
2 As far as I'm concerned
3 Elicit a few answers.

Study skills   page 77

Academic writing style

Aim
This section provides a short introduction to academic writing style. After reading a sample and focusing on some of the main features, students have an opportunity to develop a more academic style by replacing words and phrases in a text. This will help them with their IELTS writing tasks but will also be very useful preparation for their future studies in other academic contexts.

1 Ask students to read the two texts to decide whether the overall content is similar or different. Also elicit which one they think is more academic in style. Elicit some examples but don't go into details as exercise 2 covers this.

Answers
1 the same information is given in both texts
2 text A

2 Students choose the word in italics which reflects an academic writing style. Refer back to the texts in exercise 1 for specific examples.

Answers
1 formal (*One of the consequences ... is also a requirement for a number of professions ...*)
2 doesn't
3 passive (*... it is thought ..., it is spoken ...*)
4 fewer
5 doesn't
6 doesn't

3 Clarify that the sentences 1–4 make up the next paragraph of the text in exercise 1 (the more informal version). Explain that students need to replace the underlined words or phrases with the words in brackets at the end of each sentence. No further words are necessary. Do the first one as an example.

Answers
1 worldwide; on a daily basis
2 appears; constantly; the media
3 Therefore; those; claim; do not; may recognize; some; vocabulary
4 Similarly; such as; globally; due to; large

4 Elicit why the passive voice is more appropriate for sentences 1 and 4 and ask students to rewrite these using the passive.

Answers
because the agent refers to people in general
1 English is heard or spoken worldwide on a daily basis.
4 Similarly, names such as McDonald's and Starbucks are recognized globally due to the spread of large multinational companies.

Suggestion
Continue to emphasize the importance of academic writing style by highlighting key points or errors in any written tasks your students do.

Content overview

Themes

This unit is based on the topic of technology and focuses on robots, various gadgets and how a hot air balloon works.

Exam related activities

Reading

Locating information
Multiple choice

Writing

Task 1   Describing how a hot air balloon/a fire extinguisher work
Organizing your answer
Expressing purpose

Listening

Section 4   Table completion
Multiple choice
Note completion

Speaking

Describing listening habits
Part 2   Describing an item of technology
Part 3   Discussing modern technology

Language development

Expressing purpose
Dependent prepositions
Describing objects
Vocabulary: word building

Skills development

Reading

Scanning

Study skills

Editing
Phrasal verbs with different meanings

Reading   pages 78–80

Aim

This section gives students practice in locating specific information and detail by reading a text about modern technology.

1 Elicit which products/inventions are shown and find out how many of these are owned by the class. Initiate a discussion about which of the inventions they find most useful and would find it hard to live without.

Alternatively, you could conduct a mini class survey to find out how many of the inventions mentioned in the text are owned/used on a regular basis.

2 Elicit which of the inventions listed they think was invented first and last. Do not tell them the answers yet but ask them to match inventions and dates (encourage guesswork!) and then briefly compare their answers with their partner. Students then quickly read the text to locate the answers. You could give them a time limit to encourage speed reading.

Answers

1892: trainers
1949: bar codes
1970s: TV dinners
1978: GPS technology
1979: Sony Walkman®
1994: PlayStation™

3 Ask students to work in pairs to discuss the questions before having a whole-class discussion. Encourage students to compare their ideas and justify their opinions. You could mention that the first and third questions are similar to ones they might get in Speaking Part 3.

4 Locating information

Questions 1–7

Tell students that they have to match the information to a paragraph in the text. Encourage them to underline key words in the questions and then highlight words or phrases in the text that have similar meanings.

Answers

1 B (*This wearable technology has now evolved, thanks to Apple®, into the iPod® ...*)
2 F (*... more than three billion minutes are spent by computer users on Facebook.*)
3 E (*The gaming industry is now worth almost as much as the film industry ...*)
4 J (*With the help of celebrity endorsements ...*)
5 C (*Norman Woodland first developed an early form of the bar code ...*)
6 I (*... while the US military has developed a 'less-than-lethal' weapon ...*)
7 A (*... while conservation scientists have tagged turtles with GPS receivers ...*)

Multiple choice

There are three different types of multiple-choice question in this section: the first requiring just one answer from a choice of four, the second requiring two answers from a choice of five, and the final part requiring three answers from a choice of eight. Check that students understand that for questions 9–10 and 11–13 the order of the answers is not important. Encourage students to underline key words and to be aware of distracters.

Answers

Question 8
B
Questions 9–10
B (para H: *... the ability to spend money anywhere in the world.*); E (para F: *Online social networking has allowed people to rekindle friendships with friends they lost touch with years ago.*) (in any order)
Questions 11–13
A (para G: *... that is almost incomprehensible to those who do not use it*); F (para H: *They also brought us ... record levels of debt ...*); G (para D: *... the diet of the Western world has deteriorated.*) (in any order)

Language focus   pages 80–81

Dependent prepositions

Aim
Using the correct dependent preposition is a common area of difficulty and this exercise encourages students to focus on which prepositions are used in certain verb phrases in the context of technology. There is further practice of dependent prepositions in the Grammar and vocabulary bank on page 155.

1 Ask students individually to complete the sentences with the correct prepositions before checking their

answers with the text. You may want to encourage the use of dictionaries to check dependent prepositions.

Answers

1 on, with	3 to	5 to
2 for	4 with	6 with

Expressing purpose

Aim
The exercises in this section focus on an area which is particularly useful in Task 1 of the Writing exam. This has already been touched on in Unit 6 and will be looked at later in this unit in the context of describing how something works.

2 Lead in to this section by referring students back to the text on page 79 and asking them questions: *Why was the bar code created? What are sports stars used for?*, etc. This should get students thinking about how we use this type of language. Then ask them to match the sentence halves.

Answers

1 c	2 a	3 d	4 f	5 b	6 e

3 Encourage students to use the sentences from the previous exercise to complete the grammar rules. You may like to do an example together to help them.

Answers

1 *-ing* form	4 infinitive
2 subject + verb	5 infinitive
3 infinitive	

4 Students use the expressions in brackets to form a link between the two sentences. Monitor to ensure they are using the correct form after the expression of purpose. Refer them to the grammar rules in exercise 3.

Answers

1 People use credit and debit cards so that they can shop online safely.
2 People use personal stereos when travelling so as not to disturb other people.
3 TV dinners are often frozen so as to be easy to prepare quickly.
4 People like wearing trainers to be comfortable and fashionable.
5 Personal stereos are small and light in order to be portable.
6 Microwave ovens use microwave radiation for cooking food.

5 Demonstrate the activity to the class by telling them the purpose of an object in the classroom. Give them clues until they guess the object. Then refer them to the written example. As they do the task in pairs, monitor to check that they are using appropriate ways to express purpose.

IELTS Writing Task 1: Describing how something works

Aim

This section focuses on describing how something works using information provided in a diagram and is a possible task in IELTS Writing Task 1. It incorporates ways of expressing purpose, reviewing language covered in the previous Language focus section.

1 Ask students how they would feel about travelling in a hot air balloon or if anyone has had this experience. Elicit any comments on how hot air balloons might work.

2 Ask students to check any unknown words in their dictionaries. Refer students to the pictures and ask them to complete the labels in the relevant parts of the drawing. In pairs, students discuss how a hot air balloon works using the information shown in the diagram. One or two pairs could perform their discussion to the class. Minimal correction is necessary as this is mainly oral preparation for tasks to come.

Answers

a	basket	e	gas burner
b	steel ropes	f	jets of flame
c	nylon	g	safety harness
d	vehicle	h	valve

3 Ask students what information they should include in the first sentence of their answer (introductory statement expressing the function or purpose of the object). Then get them to reorder the jumbled sentence to form an appropriate introductory statement.

Answer

A hot air balloon is used for sport and leisure and usually carries up to four people./A hot air balloon usually carries up to four people and is used for sport and leisure.

4 Students read the model answer and complete the text with the correct verb forms. In feedback elicit and highlight the use of the present simple, both active and passive to describe how something works.

Answers

1	consists of	6	to launch
2	stand	7	heats
3	made of	8	rises
4	is attached	9	to wear
5	is inflated	10	controls

Organizing your answer

5 This exercise highlights the clear structure of the model answer by getting students to match each paragraph to its purpose. Emphasize that a well-organized answer is always important.

Answers

1 third paragraph
2 first paragraph
3 second paragraph

Expressing purpose

6 See how many expressions of purpose students can remember from earlier in the unit. Then get them to locate and underline the expressions in the model answer.

Answers

so as to be ..., so as not to ..., is used to ..., in order to ..., so that

7 Look at the example together and highlight how using an expression of purpose can make the style of students' writing more academic and that it provides vital information in this type of task. Encourage students to use a different expression of purpose to improve each sentence.

Suggested answers

1 Balloons are usually bright colours so as to be easily visible.
2 Mobile phones are small and light so that people can carry them in pockets or handbags.
3 Modern computers have large memories in order to store many files.

Practice

8 Students read the rubric and look at the diagram. Encourage them to describe the process orally to a partner and to check any unknown vocabulary in a dictionary.

9 These questions are aimed at getting the students to think about key questions so they can structure their answers in a logical order.

Answers

Students' own answers from the diagram.

10 Having completed the previous activities, this task could be set as a timed-writing activity in class or for homework. Give feedback as necessary.

Answer

See model answer on page 162.

Describing objects

Aim

In both the writing and speaking parts of the IELTS exam, students may be asked to describe an object. This section gives them the opportunity to build their vocabulary in this area.

1 To lead in to this section you could try to elicit the categories in the table (shape, size, structure, etc.) by asking students to describe some simple classroom objects. Then get students to complete the table with the words and expressions in the box.

Answers

Shape	Size	Structure	Material	Colour

It is …
flat
cylindrical
round
	It is …
	1 metre in
	  diameter
	10 cm high/
	  long/wide/
	  deep
	bigger/
	  smaller than
	  a …
	the size of a …
	tiny
		It contains …
		It consists
		  of …
		two parts
		three
		  sections
			It's made of …
			It is…
			leather
			metal
			plastic
			wooden
				It is …
				a shade of
				  pink
				light/dark
				  brown
				metallic grey

2 Encourage students to add more examples to each column. If they are having difficulty here, you could help them by asking prompt questions: *What is your scarf made of? What shape is your notebook?*

3 Demonstrate the activity by describing a classroom object using some of the vocabulary from the previous activity. Then put students in pairs and get them to choose a few objects to describe. Monitor closely and give feedback.

Speaking   page 85

Aim

This section gives students the opportunity to use some of the language from the previous exercises and also introduces them to the type of visual data that is sometimes found in Task 1 of the Writing exam, where students are required to describe an object or the stages in the development of something.

1 These first questions reflect the type of questions students may be asked in Part 1 of the Speaking exam. Students ask and answer the questions in pairs. Encourage them to give extended answers and provide reasons.

2 Ask students to identify the four different types of music format and see which ones they are familiar with/have

used. (The answers to this may largely depend on the age of your students.) Point out that information about each of the formats is provided in the boxes A–D. Ask students to check any unknown vocabulary in their dictionaries and then match each box to the relevant picture. Students work in pairs to describe and compare the different formats. Encourage them to be creative here and add some of their own ideas, as well as using expressions from the vocabulary section.

Answers

B: Long-playing record (LP)
D: Cassette tape
C: Compact disc (CD)
A: MP3 player

The Study skills section on page 89 provides a Writing Task 1 rubric and sample answer for these pictures.

Listening   pages 86–87

IELTS Listening Section 4

Aim

This is a Part 4 Listening module text, ie an academic lecture. As this is the most challenging section for students and as they only hear the text once in the actual exam, it is important to build their confidence in class.

1 In pairs or small groups, ask students to look at the pictures and discuss the different types of robots. Give students a few minutes to discuss the questions in pairs before brief class feedback.

Answers

Students' own answers.

2 Table completion

Questions 1–5

 Give students some time to look at the table and predict the type of answer they should be listening for.

Answers

1	help him walk	4	1801
2	write messages	5	mathematical operations
3	Vaucanson		

In today's lecture I want to give you a brief overview of the history of robotics, from ancient times up to the present day. We can then look at some of the key inventions in more detail over the next few weeks.

You may have wondered why I mentioned ancient times. Aren't robots a modern invention? Well, technically, yes, but ancient civilizations had very similar ideas, for example, there was the story of Talos, a man made from bronze, who guarded the island of Crete, in Greece. Then in Roman mythology the god Vulcan made two female robots out of gold to help him walk.

However, by 1774 myth had become fact, and two French brothers, Pierre and Henri Louis Jacquet-Droz were creating very complicated automatons, such as a boy robot, which could draw and write messages. They also created a robot woman, which could play a piano. Another example was a mechanical duck, which quacked, flapped its wings and pretended to eat and drink. This was invented at about the same time, by a man called Vaucanson. That's V–A–U–C–A–N–S–O–N.

In the next century robots started to be designed which were not so much toys, but had more practical, industrial uses. The industrial robots used in factories today have their origins in these early automated machines.

A good example is Joseph Jacquard's Textile Machine, invented in 1801 which was operated by punch cards.

Then, in 1834, Charles Babbage designed one of the first automatic computers, the Analytic Engine. This also used programs on punched cards to carry out mathematical operations. It had a memory capable of one thousand 50 digit numbers. The project was never finished, but it provided an excellent model for later developments.

Multiple choice and Note completion

Questions 6–8 and Questions 9–10

 2.4 In this listening exercise, a range of question types is used, as is normal in IELTS. Explain to students that listening texts are usually split up into two parts, and they will be given a short amount of time in the exam to look ahead at the questions before each part. You could also mention that students get half a minute to check their answers after each section (as well as the 10 minutes transfer time at the end). Before listening to the second part of the lecture, give students time to read the questions. Ensure students understand that two answers are required for questions 6–7. Ensure that students understand that questions 9–10 require them to write three words or fewer for each answer.

Answers

6/7	B, E
8	C
9	world leader
10	hydrogen fuel cells

2.4

The 20th century was a time which saw huge development in the science of robotics, particularly after the computer had been developed in the mid-forties. George Devol designed the Universal Automaton in 1954, which was the first programmable robot. The name was later shortened to Unimaton, which became the name of the first robot company.

Unimaton Inc sold designs to General Motors, who, in 1962, installed the first industrial robot on a production line. The

'Unimate' robot was used in a car factory to lift and stack hot pieces of metal.

In 1970, a computer-controlled robot called Shakey was developed. On one occasion Shakey was asked to push a box off a platform. It couldn't reach the box, so it found a ramp, pushed the ramp against the platform, rolled up the ramp and pushed the box to the floor. Doesn't that seem like intelligence?

Since then hundreds of robots have been designed and developed for a variety of uses: assembling small parts in factories, providing the handicapped with artificial limbs, carrying out household chores and even carrying out surgical operations.

In 1967 Japan imported its first industrial robot from the United States, which was, at this time, about ten years ahead in robot technology. However, within a very short time, Japan started to catch up and then take over. Japan is now a world leader in robotics. Sony's Aibo robot dog was the first sophisticated robotic product to really sell well to the public. Now Honda have created Asimo, who has been made two-legged, in order to look more human. He is designed as 'a partner for people', or to work in the home. Asimo became the first non-human to open the New York Stock Exchange. Asimo will continue to be developed and, in the future, its power may come from hydrogen fuel cells, a technology whose only waste product is water. This may mean that Asimo will have to go to the toilet!

If these plans work out then society in the future could be very different. In fifty years time, perhaps, no home or workplace will be without one.

Vocabulary   page 87

Aim

These exercises provide students with further practice in identifying and using different parts of speech and building word families from root words.

1 Ask students to read the sentences in exercise 2 and identify the word class of each of the missing words. Check as a class.

Answers

1	noun	5	noun	8	verb
2	adverb	6	noun	9	noun
3	verb	7	noun	10	adjective
4	noun				

2 Students use the word in brackets to form a new word to complete the sentence. Encourage students to use dictionaries to check their answers before whole-class feedback.

Answers

1	developments	6	design
2	creatively	7	manufacturers
3	invented	8	equipped
4	width	9	weight
5	production	10	cylindrical

Refer students to the Grammar and vocabulary bank on page 155, where there is further practice of synonyms of *make* and collocations with *make* and *do*.

IELTS Speaking Part 2

Suggestion
To add variety to this Part 2 activity you could bring some realia into class, eg camera, MP3 player, Swiss Army Knife, etc., and give a short talk about that specific object based on the prompts on the card. Alternatively, you could find visuals of different objects or appliances, distribute them and ask each student to do the task relating to the picture they have been given.

1 The students have had quite a bit of input in this unit to help them with this task. Using word maps like this is a useful way of generating ideas and vocabulary and can be used for writing as well as speaking tasks. Once the students have completed their word map, they can use it as a prompt to do the task. Get them to do this in pairs, with one student timing and giving feedback to their partner before swapping roles.

IELTS Speaking Part 3

2 This exercise gives students time to formulate ideas in note form. Although students do not get time for this in the exam, it is a useful skill and will give them support whilst practising the most difficult part of the speaking exam.

3 Once students have made their notes, get them working in pairs to ask and answer the questions. Encourage them to use their notes as prompts and to expand them with reasons and examples. Monitor and give specific feedback.

Study skills   page 89

Editing

Aim
This exercise aims to consolidate and practise work introduced in the Study skills section of Unit 3 and to emphasize the importance of accuracy in academic writing. It also introduces students to a rubric and sample answer for a Writing Task 1, which requires them to describe the development of an object over time.

1 Refer students back to the pictures on page 85 and ask them to read the rubric for the Writing task. Students then read the sample answer and locate the six underlined mistakes and correct them. The final two paragraphs of the answer contain six further mistakes,

which are not underlined. Ask students to underline these as they find them and then correct them.

Answers
1 correct forms in brackets
    There has been (plural: have been)
    records invented (passive: were invented)
    flat, circle objects (adjective: circular)
    30cm daimeter (spelling: diameter)
    These are consisted of (active: consisted of)
    considerable (adverb: considerably)
2 correct forms in brackets
    Compact discs have appeared (past simple: appeared)
    ... more smaller (comparative form: smaller)
    people listened music (verb + preposition: listened to music)
    that are small items (non-defining relative pronoun: which)
    designed fitting into (verb + infinitive: designed to fit into)
    thousands of song (plural: songs)

Phrasal verbs with different meanings

Aim
Phrasal verbs are an area of language that can cause students many difficulties with both meaning and grammar. The exercises here focus on two phrasal verbs which appear in the text on page 79 and aim to raise students' awareness of how phrasal verbs can have two or more different meanings. Refer students to the Grammar and vocabulary bank on page 155, where there is further practice of using phrasal verbs with pronouns.

2 Refer students back to the text on page 79 and ask them to find the two phrasal verbs in context and choose from the three alternative meanings. Make sure that students understand that the other two meanings are also correct in different contexts and be prepared to give examples to show them this.

Answers
1 b
2 b

3 Ask students to read the sentences and to try to guess the meaning of the phrasal verbs from the context. They can then check their answers by using their dictionaries to look up the phrasal verbs.

Answers
1 understand
2 improving

Content overview

Themes

The topic of the unit is health and medicine and covers topics such as alternative therapies, illnesses and diseases and healthy lifestyles.

Exam related activities

Reading

Classification
True, False, Not Given
Summary completion
Multiple choice

Writing

Task 2   Alternative medicine
Key phrases to express impersonal views
Preparing to write
Using an appropriate writing style
Using adverbs

Listening

Section 3   Multiple choice
Note completion

Speaking

Part 3   Discussing health and healthcare

Language development

Vocabulary: parts of the body and illnesses/conditions; health and medical breakthroughs
Real conditionals
Unreal conditionals

Study skills

Avoiding repetition

Reading   pages 90–92

1 Ask students to use the dictionary definition to elicit the difference(s) between conventional and alternative medicine.

Suggested answers

Alternative medicine uses different methods from conventional medicine, often involving techniques such as massage, acupuncture, etc., with the emphasis on treating the whole person rather than curing the disease or illness with drugs or surgery.

2 Put students into pairs and ask them to decide which statements they think are conventional or alternative therapies. Note that the concept 'alternative medicine' is taken from a Western perspective and that many of the methods referred to may well be more common in certain cultures, eg Chinese.

Suggested answers

Conventional: 1, 3, 4
Alternative: 2, 5, 6

3 Ask students to discuss the question in pairs and/or as a class.

4 Classification

Questions 1–5
Students may ask for the meanings of the four types of alternative therapy before reading, but these will become clear from the text. Ask the students to look through the descriptions and then read the text to find out which therapies are being described. Point out that classification is similar to matching. However, the headings or classifications can be used more than once.

Answers

1 I (*This therapy was invented in the early nineteenth century by ...*)
2 A (*... patients treated with acupuncture ... had less intense pain than patients who received a placebo.*)
3 C (*A chiropractor manipulates joints ...*)
4 I (*... the eye markings can reveal a complete history of past illnesses.*)
5 R (*... It is now possible to buy reflexology guides and foot massagers for do-it-yourself reflexology.*)

True, False, Not given

Questions 6–9

All the statements are claims and opinions of various experts and practitioners. Ask students to read the statements carefully and then look in the text to find evidence for their choices.

> **Suggestion**
> These questions are based on the opinions of key people in the text. Encourage the students to look for and underline their names (Professor Ernst, Dr Barrett and Practitioners) as a way of finding the answers, but make sure they check carefully by reading the sentences around the names.

Answers

6 F (*There is good clinical evidence that acupuncture works for … dental … pain.*)
7 NG (Researchers found there was no evidence that it helps with asthma, but the text does not state that practitioners claim that it does.)
8 T (*There is no scientific support for these assertions.*)
9 T (*Patients and therapists should be discouraged from using this method.*)

Summary completion

Questions 10–13

Ask students to read the summary and identify which part of the text they will need to focus on to find the answers (Chiropractic manipulation). Make sure that students realize that they should use one or two words from the text. Encourage them to find synonyms of key words in the summary (eg *increase mobility* in the summary appears as – *improve mobility* in the text).

Answers

10 mobility	12 ineffective
11 most dangerous	13 limited

Multiple choice

Question 14

This question tests students' global understanding of the text. Having completed questions 1–13, they should have a fairly good idea so only give them a short time to answer this question.

Answer

14 D

5 In small groups, students discuss which of the methods described in the text they would be willing to try and why/why not. They can also talk about the techniques which they have experienced.

6 Ask students to describe other alternative therapies they may have experienced, eg aromatherapy, etc.

Vocabulary   page 92

Parts of the body and illnesses/conditions

1 Individually, ask students to scan the text and underline parts of the body. Only give a short time for this before comparing answers.

Answers

Acupuncture: back
Reflexology: hands, feet, nerves, blood, lungs
Iridology: eye
Chiropractic manipulation: spine, joints, hands, nerves, brain, neck, vertebral artery, back

2 Students work in pairs to match the illnesses/conditions in the left column with the parts of the body in the right. Students can use dictionaries to check any unknown words. Then check as a class.

Answers

1 d   2 a   3 e   4 c   5 b

3 Students match verbs with nouns to make common collocations.

Answers

to relieve: pain, symptoms
to prescribe: antibiotics, medicine
to diagnose: an illness, a condition
to treat: an illness, pain, a condition, symptoms

Refer students to the Grammar and vocabulary bank on page 156, where there is further practice of these collocations.

Language focus   page 93

Real conditionals

1 Lead in to this section by generating a discussion about colds. Ask students to read the text to see if their ideas are similar.

2 Focus students' attention on the underlined sentences in the text in exercise 1 and ask them to complete the first Result in the table. At this point you could start checking understanding of meaning by asking if we are talking about something which is always true or only

likely to be true. Students then complete the remaining gaps in the table by referring to the text.

Answers

1 symptoms include a runny nose.
2 When you catch a cold,
3 you will increase your chances of catching a cold.
4 When you cough or sneeze,
5 you should see a doctor.

3 This exercise highlights the difference in meaning between the zero and first conditionals.

Answers

likely but not definite: first
definite and always true: zero

4 This exercise focuses on the form of the two conditionals. Ask students to refer to the sentences in the table in exercise 2 to complete the table here. Next, they answer the two questions. Be prepared to show further examples if necessary.

Answers

| Zero conditional | *If/When* + present simple, | present simple |
| First conditional | *If/When* + present simple, | *will/can/should* + infinitive |

1 yes
2 comma is omitted if the order is reversed

5 Look at the examples together and use them to further check understanding by eliciting which is zero and which is first conditional. Then ask them to write their own sentences using the other prompts.

Suggested answers

1 ... it hurts a lot.
   ... you will have to go to hospital.
2 When you go to the dentist, ...
   If you cut yourself, ...
3 he/she should go to the doctor.
   he/she might need to take time off work.
4 If you are unwell, ...
   When you are pregnant, ...

Refer students to the Grammar and vocabulary bank on page 156, where there is further practice of real conditional forms.

Health and medical breakthroughs

Aim

The topic of health and medicine often occurs in the IELTS exam and this section aims to build students' vocabulary in this area. Ask students to describe the pictures and elicit ideas about healthy/unhealthy lifestyles. Encourage them to use dictionaries to check answers as they complete the table.

Answers

Types of illness and disease	Causes of ill health and disease	Ways of keeping healthy	Medical breakthroughs
cancer HIV/AIDS stress-related illness viral epidemics	a poor diet a sedentary lifestyle lack of health education poor hygiene and sanitation	a balanced diet having leisure and relaxation time keeping your mind active regular exercise	immunization infertility treatment organ transplantation stem cell research

Speaking   page 94

IELTS Speaking Part 3

Encourage students to use some of the vocabulary from the previous section to answer these questions. Give them a few minutes to note down some ideas before putting them in pairs to ask and answer the questions. In the feedback slot you could highlight strong answers or give your own responses to the questions.

Listening   page 95

IELTS Listening Section 3

Suggestion

This text is an IELTS Listening module Section 3, and includes three speakers in a seminar situation. One of the big difficulties for students with this kind of text is identifying all of the speakers. Point out clues such as gender and signposting of names by other members of the group, eg *Alice, what are your views on reproductive cloning?*

Multiple choice

Questions 1–4

(O) **2.5** Before listening, tell students that there are three people involved in the seminar. Elicit the names

(*Barry, Alice*) and ask who they think the third person is (the tutor), then ask the students what they know about cloning. Allow students time to read the questions and underline key words. You might want to pre-teach some of the vocabulary, eg *artificial, reproductive, clones, identical, therapeutic, kidney, transplanting*.

Answers

| 1 B | 2 C | 3 A | 4 B | 5/6 B, E (in any order) |

 2.5

[T =Tutor; B = Barry; A = Alice]

T: Thank you, Barry. As you said at the start of your presentation, human cloning is creating a genetically identical copy of another person and although this happens naturally, as you also mentioned, in the form of identical twins, <u>the main topic we're discussing today is artificial human cloning</u>. Alice, could you remind us of the two main types of cloning that Barry covered?

A: Yes, of course. Therapeutic cloning involves the creation of new cells or organs, embryos for example, for medical or research purposes. Reproductive cloning is actually growing a new human being.

T: And do you think that ethically there is really any difference between the two? Barry?

B: It's a good question, and I'm not really sure that I know the answer. <u>Reproductive cloning is often the one that people fear.</u> If you ask me, the idea of making a new person identical to someone living or who has lived, is a bit too close to science fiction.

T: Alice, what are your views on reproductive cloning?

A: Yes, it's true. People think of armies of clones, all the same, non-thinking machines, almost, who could be used in an attack by some mad dictator. There are so many books and films on this theme that people seem to imagine that it could really happen.

T: And couldn't it?

A: I don't think so. In my view, just because you have the same genes as someone, doesn't mean you're going to act like a robot. <u>What about identical twins? They don't do the same thing all the time but act as individuals, so I think clones would be more like that.</u>

B: Fair point. Twins have different personalities so it's unrealistic to think that clones would necessarily behave in the same way.

T: So, Barry, is there a positive side to reproductive cloning? I mean would it be beneficial to anybody?

B: Childless couples. As far as I know, if reproductive cloning were legalized, those with fertility problems could have children.

T: That's a good point. So let's turn now to therapeutic cloning. What are your thoughts on that?

A: The possibilities are fascinating. <u>If you could grow a new heart, kidney or lung for someone,</u> you would address the problem of organ shortages. At the moment, people needing transplants usually have to wait for someone who wants to donate an organ and who has the same blood and tissue type.

B: Also, <u>therapeutic cloning could be used to fight some degenerative diseases,</u> you know, the type that get worse as you get older, such as Parkinson's.

T: So, going back to the question I asked at the beginning regarding the ethical issues ...

B: I think that therapeutic cloning is easier for most people to accept as you're only talking about carrying out research on certain parts of a human, whereas reproductive cloning deals with making a complete human being, one that can think, feel and talk. Now, that's an entirely different matter.

Note completion

Questions 7–10

 2.6 Before listening to the second section of the talk, give students time to read the notes and predict the type of answers needed in each gap. Again, you might need to pre-teach some vocabulary from this section, eg *miscarriages, embryos*.

Answers

7 religious and political
8 cloned mammal
9 side effects
10 adult skin

 2.6

[T =Tutor; B = Barry; A = Alice]

T: So what do you think are the main barriers to progress or future developments in this area of medical science?

A: Well, as we touched on earlier, human cloning's always going to be a controversial topic, particularly with certain <u>religious and political groups</u> who have serious ethical concerns. Many people have real issues about artificially creating human beings and the whole notion of 'playing God', as they feel it contradicts nature. If you cloned humans, we wouldn't be unique is one of the key moral arguments against cloning.

B: That's true. Also, I think there are a number of significant issues relating to safety. If you remember, there were over 250 attempts to create Dolly the sheep, <u>the first cloned mammal,</u> and before a human being is successfully created it's highly likely there would be miscarriages, deformities or other <u>side effects</u>.

T: But isn't science all about challenging, experimenting and testing the limits of knowledge in the quest for progress?

B: Yes, you're right and there's no doubt there are benefits in terms of medical advances in this field, but at the same time there's always going to be strong opposition.

A: Yet it's not stopping people carrying out research in this area. We know that human leg cells have already been cloned and human embryos have also been created from <u>adult skin cells,</u> so developments in human cloning are happening now and will continue to happen whether we like it or not.

T: Ah yes, the inevitable march of progress. All interesting stuff. Right, let's move on to discuss ...

Unreal conditionals

1 Look at the table and tell students that the sentences are taken from the Listening on page 95. Ask them to match the sentence halves together, checking their answers with the audioscript on pages 171–172.

Answers

1 c   2 a   3 b

2 These questions check understanding of the meaning/use and form of the conditional sentences. Ensure students refer to the sentences in the table as they discuss the questions in pairs. Check answers as a class. Point out that the correct form of the verb *be* in the *If* clause is *were*, but many native speakers use *was*.

Answers

1 past simple (*could* is the past form of *can*)
2 no; the past tense refers to a hypothetical or unlikely present/future
3 *would/could* + infinitive
4 yes

3 Look at the example together and highlight the fact that the situation in the prompt is real and that the students need to use these to make unreal or hypothetical statements. Ask students to write some unreal conditional sentences using the prompts. Elicit examples in feedback.

Possible answers

1 If there were more organ donors, there wouldn't be a shortage of organs for transplantation.
   There wouldn't be a shortage of organs for transplantation if there were more organ donors.
2 If hygiene and sanitation in developing countries were better, there wouldn't be as much disease.
   There wouldn't be as much disease in developing countries if hygiene and sanitation were better.
3 If we didn't have global air travel, disease wouldn't spread so quickly around the world.
   Disease wouldn't spread so quickly around the world if we didn't have global air travel.
4 If people led healthier lifestyles, there wouldn't be so many/would be fewer cases of heart disease.
   There wouldn't be so many/would be fewer cases of heart disease if people led healthier lifestyles.
5 If we didn't have fertility treatments, there would be more childless couples.
   There would be more childless couples if we didn't have fertility treatments.

4 Now ask students to write their own sentences, either giving their opinion or simply using their imaginations.

Possible answers

If everyone was immunized against common diseases, there would be fewer deaths.
If scientists found a cure for HIV/AIDS, it would be a significant medical breakthrough.
If smoking was/were banned completely, fewer people would get lung cancer.

Refer students to the Grammar and vocabulary bank on page 156, where there is further practice of unreal conditional forms.

Writing   pages 97–100

IELTS Writing Task 2: Key phrases to express impersonal views

Aim

Although strong IELTS answers do not always need to be in a formal academic style, they do need to be balanced, well-argued and well-expressed. Impersonal phrases (*It is often said …*, *many people believe that …*) are often regarded as more appropriate in academic essays than personalized sentences. This section focuses on developing a more impersonal, academic style.

1 After looking at the three categories and the example, students read the phrases and categorize each one. After the activity, emphasize that giving first person advice, using rhetorical questions, contractions or question tags (see Tip box) is not usually appropriate when writing academic essays. However, it should be stressed that generally, in an IELTS Task 2 answer, personal phrases such as *I strongly believe …* or *In my view …*, etc. are acceptable.

Answers

1 C – use of direct question is inappropriate in writing
2 A – appropriate use of impersonal style
3 B – personal opinion using *I* but appropriate in an IELTS Task 2 essay
4 A – appropriate use of impersonal style.
5 B – personal opinion using *I* but appropriate in an IELTS Task 2 essay
6 C – use of rhetorical question and informal expression inappropriate in writing
7 A – appropriate use of impersonal style.

2 Students consider the contexts and select an appropriate style for each one.

Answers

1 semi-formal	4 semi-formal
2 informal	5 formal or semi-formal
3 formal	6 informal

3 Students look at the language used in the sentences and match them to the situations in exercise 2.

Answers

a 4   b 1   c 2   d 5   e 6   f 3

Preparing to write

4 After reading the sample Task 2 question (possibly underlining key words) students answer the key questions individually or in pairs. This exercise aims to check understanding of the question, helps to generate ideas and encourages students to make a brief outline before writing their answer. Other tasks in the unit should serve as input for this stage. Conduct brief feedback. Students then skim read the sample to compare their own ideas with the main points in the text, ignoring the gaps at this point.

Answers

Students' own answers.

Using an appropriate writing style

5 Next, students select the best option for each gap in the text then check with their partner. In the feedback stage clarify which form is the most suitable for each gap and why making sure that a more academic, impersonal style is the target (avoidance of phrasal verbs, contractions, etc.). See Study Skills section Unit 6 page 77.

Answers

1 A	3 B	5 C	7 A	9 C
2 C	4 A	6 B	8 C	10 A

Practice

6 Go through the example statement followed by the impersonal and more personal opinions. Students write their own answers for the three statements. Remind them to provide suitable reasons.

Suggested answers

1 Many people believe that nurses should have much higher salaries as they work long hours and also do shift work.
  In my opinion, nurses should earn more money as they work long hours and also do shift work.

2 Many people would argue that not everyone should pay for their own healthcare as many cannot afford it and this should be the responsibility of the state.
  I am unconvinced that everyone should pay for their own healthcare as many cannot afford it and this should be the responsibility of the state.

3 The majority of people would consider that a hospital is the best place to recover from an illness as there are well-trained staff and appropriate healthcare facilities.
  I am absolutely certain that a hospital is the best place to recover from an illness as there are well-trained staff and appropriate healthcare facilities.

Using adverbs

7 This section offers another way for students to express their opinions more indirectly. Look at the two example sentences from the sample answer on page 98 and elicit the answer to the first question (what the writer thinks). Ask students to look at the adverbs in the box and match them with the questions.

Answers

what the writer thinks
1 apparently
2 unfortunately
3 fortunately
4 surprisingly
5 clearly, naturally, obviously

8 Ask students to use the adverbs from the box in exercise 7 to complete the sentences. Different answers are possible but stress that this depends on the writer's opinion. Students do this individually, and then compare and discuss their answers.

Suggested answers

1 Obviously/Clearly/Naturally
2 Surprisingly/Apparently/Naturally
3 Apparently/Unfortunately
4 Unfortunately/Obviously/Clearly
5 Surprisingly/Apparently/Unfortunately
6 Apparently

Suggestion
Although adverbs can come in different places in a sentence, eg following the subject, for the sake of ease and clarity students could be encouraged to always use them at the beginning of a sentence, as in this exercise.

9 This section gives further practice of IELTS Writing Task 2. Ask students to read the question then consider the strategy below as a guideline for approaching this type of task. Allow them time to understand the question and to decide how much they agree or disagree with the statement. Emphasize that a clear opinion (agreeing or disagreeing with the statement) is expected but that a balanced argument would be appropriate too. Students may want to discuss the task in pairs or small groups before writing their answer. The essay may be written as a timed-writing activity in class, or for homework.

Answer

See model answer on pages 162–163.

Study skills   page 101

Avoiding repetition

Aim

This section aims to raise students' awareness of referencing in order to help them understand more complex texts, as well as to improve the style of their own writing. Similar activities could be done with any text they read.

1 Ask students to read the short text about acupuncture. Elicit that the underlined words and phrases are too repetitive and could be replaced by other words. See if students can offer any suggestions for appropriate reference words here.

Answers

Acupuncture: The practice/It/which (continuing first sentence)
In China: there, in that country
The practitioners: They
the forces of yin and yang: these

2 Having looked at the example, ask students to find what is referred to by underlining or drawing arrows. Point out that the use of too many referencing words can also have a negative effect and make a text difficult to follow.

Answers

there: in the lining of the respiratory passages
This: something (which should not be there)
them: the lungs
this: dirt or dust (getting into the lungs)
them: the lungs
it: coughing
this: trying not to cough
it: trying not to cough

3 Ask the students to replace the underlined sections with reference links as shown in the example.

Answers

1 They	4 one; this
2 They; they	5 it; then
3 This; it	6 These

4 You could take specific examples from student essays you have recently marked (anonymously) or ask students to identify passages of their own to rewrite to improve cohesion and avoid repetition.

Content overview

Themes

This unit explores the theme of intelligence, looking in particular at animal intelligence and the idea of multiple intelligences.

Exam related activities

Reading

Note completion

Writing

Task 2   Organization and coherence: paragraphing

Listening

Section 4   Summary completion
                  Multiple choice with more than one option
Section 3   Note completion

Speaking

Part 2
Describing a time when you learned something new

Part 3

Discussing learning environments and kinds of intelligence

Language development

Signs of intelligence
-ing form and infinitive
Lexical links
Expressions to describe skills

Skills development

Reading

Jigsaw reading and reporting back

Study skills

Hedging

Collocations focus

Mind and brain idioms

Reading   pages 102–104

Aim

This is a jigsaw reading activity, aimed at encouraging students to be able to summarize key points and exchange information as they might in a seminar situation, as well as giving practice in the IELTS task of note completion.

1 See if students can name the most intelligent animal apart from man. This will probably elicit a variety of answers, as opinion is divided on the question. Elicit some of the criteria they are using, eg *can communicate with each other, uses tools*.

Then ask students to work in groups of three to carry out tasks 1 and 2.

Possible answers

Note that this is a discussion task so there are no correct answers. There are different rankings according to different criteria. Possible rankings are:
chimp, dolphin, orang-utan, elephant, crow, pig, squirrel, pigeon, octopus, rat (see http://animal.discovery.com/tv/a-list/creature-countdowns/smartest/smartest-01.html);

chimp, gorilla, orang-utan, baboon, gibbon, monkey, smaller-toothed whale, dolphin, elephant, pig (see http://www.enotes.com/science-fact-finder/animal-world/besides-humans-which-animals-most-intelligent); great ape, dolphin, whale, monkey, elephant, crow, parrot, dog, cat, pig (see http://scienceray.com/biology/zoology/top-15-smartest-and-most-intelligent-animals/)

2/3 In the same groups of three, each student should choose a different passage (Betty, Project Delphis or Orang-utan Language Project) and read it to answer the questions. They should then share what they found out with the other members of their group.

Answers

1 Betty: to test the crow's ability to make simple tools
   Project Delphis: to find evidence that dolphins are self-aware
   Orang-utan Language Project: to test orang-utans' ability to communicate
2 Betty: make tools, use tools
   Project Delphis: recognize themselves in a mirror
   Orang-utan Language Project: read numbers and symbols

3 Betty: yes
  Project Delphis: yes
  Orang-utan Language Project: yes

Note completion

Exam information
Note completion is a similar task to the summary completion task in Unit 8. Remind students that the notes will express the same ideas as the passage, but will be paraphrased, so students need to identify the correct part of the passage (ideas will be in the same order) and then select the word or words which will fit.

4 Students read all three passages and complete the notes. Before they start refer students to the Tip. As you check answers, ask students to point out the part of the text where they found the answer.

Answers

1	lift	8	zinc oxide mark
2	bent	9	man and apes
3	nine	10	symbol
4	sticky tape	11	bell rang
5	materials	12	rewards
6	one-way mirror	13	ability to communicate
7	twisted and turned		

5 Students discuss the questions in their groups and feed back some of their ideas to the class.

Vocabulary   page 105

Aim
The aim of this section is to raise awareness of how repetition of lexis and synonyms, or lexical links, can be used to hold a text together. This should help students to understand the logic of a text better.

1 Look at the Tip together. Do the first word (*tool*) as an example, then ask students to work individually to find the other words. Check as a class. If possible, it would be helpful if you could highlight the pairs of words in the text so that students can see how they link and help the text to cohere.

Answers
Text 1: implement, bird
Text 2: creature, faculty
Text 3: carry out, selection

2 Students use their awareness of lexical links to decide which missing sentences should go where in a text. This is not an IELTS task type (though it is found in other exams), but it will help them to develop a sense of how texts cohere.

Ask students to work individually to match the sentences and paragraphs, then as you carry out feedback, ask them which links helped them to do the task.

Answers
1 B (*language, communicate, linguist*)
2 D (repetition of *the evidence*)
3 A (repetition of *level* and *argument*)
4 C (*change in classification, reclassified*)

Listening   pages 106–7

IELTS Listening Section 4

Aim
In this section, students are given the chance to listen to a lecture. The recording is longer than in previous units, but the tasks are divided into three sections. Two of these sections follow the IELTS formula, with ten questions. The third section also contains an IELTS task type.

1 Ask students to discuss the question without looking at exercise 2. They will probably find that they have different preferences.

2 Look together at the learning styles associated with their preferences. Students briefly discuss if they feel this is true for them, and the idea that different people learn in different ways.

Summary completion

Exam information
Summary completion is a similar task to sentence completion, with a summarizing paragraph rather than unconnected sentences. Note that answers must be grammatically correct, and, as with all IELTS Listening tasks, correctly spelt. The words should be taken directly from the recording and keep the same grammatical form.

3 (◎) **2.7** Draw students' attention to the Strategy box. Give them some time to read the first summary and to predict the kind of answers required (including word class). Ask them to underline key words to listen for, eg *linguistic intelligence, journalists, teachers*, etc. However, make students aware that they may hear a paraphrase rather than the exact word found in the question.

Play the recording. Note that there is a pause halfway through at *They make good scientists, computer programmers, engineers, accountants or mathematicians.*

Answers

1 words
2 persuading
3 lawyers
4 making connections
5 student
6 communicate
7 strengths and weaknesses
8 sense of direction
9 separate from intelligence/entirely separate
10 play an instrument

 2.7

[A = Announcer; JG = John Gregory]

A: As part of our series of study skills talks, John Gregory is going to talk to you today about the theory of multiple intelligences, a way of discovering more about how you, as an individual, may learn best.

JG: Hello. I'd like to start off today by giving you a little background information on the theory and then look at what these multiple intelligences are and how you can learn to make the most of your strengths in different areas.

The traditional view of intelligence, as measured by IQ tests, tends to focus on just two sorts of intelligence – Linguistic and Logical-Mathematical, or in other words being good with words or with numbers and logic. In his book *Frames of Mind*, Howard Gardner suggested that there were in fact other ways of being intelligent, that were not always recognized by the school system. He suggested seven different intelligences, which we will look at today, though he has since increased the number to eight, and thinks there may be more still.

So, what are the types of multiple intelligence? Firstly, those already mentioned. Linguistic and Logical-Mathematical. People with linguistic or verbal intelligence are good at communicating with others through words. They will learn languages easily and enjoy writing and speaking. They tend to think in words rather than in pictures. They will be good at explaining and teaching and persuading others to their point of view. Not surprisingly, they will often become journalists, teachers, lawyers, politicians and writers.

Those who are strong in Logical-Mathematical intelligence are good at seeing patterns and making connections between pieces of information. They reason well and can solve problems effectively. They're the kind of student that asks a lot of questions! They make good scientists, computer programmers, engineers, accountants or mathematicians.

[pause]

Then there are the Personal intelligences – Interpersonal, meaning between people, and Intrapersonal, meaning within yourself. Those of you with good Interpersonal intelligence have the ability to see things from other people's points of view, understanding how others feel and think. You encourage people to co-operate and communicate well with others, both verbally and non-verbally. You'll make good counsellors, salespeople, politicians and managers.

Intrapersonal intelligence is more about being able to understand yourself, recognize your own strengths and weaknesses, and your inner feelings. If you're strong in this area you'll make good researchers, theorists and philosophers.

If you tend to think in pictures rather than words, you may be strong in Visual-Spatial intelligence. You enjoy drawing and designing, as well as reading and writing. If you tend to doodle on your notes in class, that may be a sign of this intelligence. You'll have a good sense of direction and find graphs, charts and maps easy to understand. A good job for you might be a designer, an architect, a mechanic or engineer.

Bodily-Kinaesthetic intelligence is about the ability to control body movements and handle objects skilfully. Athletes, dancers, actors will be strong in this area. Sometimes physical skills are seen as something entirely separate from intelligence, something which Gardner strongly challenges by including this intelligence.

Finally, Musical intelligence. If you have a good deal of Musical intelligence you'll often play an instrument, but not necessarily. If you often find yourself tapping out rhythms in class, this may be a sign that you're learning through your Musical intelligence. Not surprisingly you'll make a good musician or songwriter.

4 To allow the students to respond to the content of the listening, let them discuss the questions in pairs or small groups, with a brief class feedback. The last question also acts as a prediction task for the last section of the listening.

Multiple choice

Exam information

In these questions more than one option has to be selected and each option correctly chosen is worth one mark.

5   **2.8** Ask the students to look through the options and make sure they know that they need to choose two activities in each case. They may be able to make some guesses, which they should confirm or disprove by listening.

Answers

1 B, C	2 A, D	3 B, D

 2.8

If you're aware of where your strengths lie, you can use this information to help you study more effectively. For example, if you have high Linguistic intelligence you'll learn well through group discussions, listening to lectures and reading, whereas if you're stronger in Logical-Mathematical intelligence you may learn better through problem-solving activities. Those of you with strong Visual-Spatial intelligence will respond well to videos, diagrams and charts. You'll probably find it helpful to learn vocabulary through using word maps.

If you are Interpersonally intelligent, try working in groups or pairs or teaching someone else what you're trying to learn. Your good communication skills mean that you'll also learn well through listening to others. Or, if you're more Intrapersonally intelligent, it may be better for you to do some studying alone, setting yourself goals.

If you have high Bodily-Kinaesthetic intelligence you may find it easy to study while walking around – though perhaps you shouldn't try this in class! The Musically intelligent may learn well through songs, or with <u>background music on while they study</u>.

It is important to recognize that everyone is a combination of all the intelligences, just in different strengths. For many tasks and jobs you need to use a combination of strengths. So, what does the questionnaire you've completed tell you about how you learn?

6 Ask students to discuss which of the items in the list they would like in their ideal classroom. Do they think that their choices reflect their learning styles?

Language focus   page 108

-ing form and infinitive

Suggestion
While this activity will make your students more aware of certain tendencies in terms of which verbs are followed by -ing or the infinitive, it is important that you encourage them to use their dictionaries to check verb patterns, and that they should include this information when recording new verbs they learn.

1 Either begin by looking at the explanation in the Grammar and vocabulary bank on page 157 together, or ask students to try and complete the sentences using either an infinitive or an -ing form, to see what they know, before looking at the grammar explanation. Clarify any problems in feedback.

Answers

1 I love visiting art galleries.
2 I dislike working alone.
3 I appreciate spending time alone.
4 ... I need to understand how something works.
5 I like learning the words of songs.
6 I would like to speak several foreign languages.

2 Check understanding by asking students to discuss together which 'intelligence' they think they represent.

Answers

0 Bodily-Kinaesthetic intelligence
1 Visual-Spatial intelligence
2 Interpersonal intelligence
3 Intrapersonal intelligence
4 Logical-Mathematical intelligence
5 Musical intelligence
6 Linguistic intelligence

3 Ask students to categorize the examples from exercise 1 by putting them into the table.

Answers

Followed by -ing:
appreciate

Followed by infinitive:
need
would like

Followed by both -ing and infinitive:
love
like
dislike
(Note that although these verbs can be followed by both forms, the infinitive is mostly used in American English.)

4 Ask students to complete these three sentences in a similar way to those in exercise 1. Elicit from them that the verbs are all followed by an -ing form because they all have a dependent preposition.

5 Now ask students to categorize the verbs in the box. Encourage them to use their dictionaries if necessary, as this is a good strategy for them to use outside the classroom. You may find it helpful to point out certain patterns or tendencies, such as verbs which convey intentions or desires (*want, decide, plan, hope, wish*) take the infinitive.

Also note that *want* and *need* can sometimes take an -ing form when the verb refers to an inanimate object, eg *Your bed needs making; The car wants servicing.* This use is colloquial.

Answers

-ing: avoid, consider, imagine, involve, mind, practise
infinitive: agree, decide, fail, hope, promise, refuse, want, wish
both: begin, forget, remember, stop, try

6 In pairs, allow students to work through the questions in order to clarify the differences in meaning. Then check answers as a class and provide any further clarification.

Answers

1 a – *like watching* is about enjoyment, in British English.
2 b – *like to learn* suggests it is a good idea or a worthwhile thing to do (eg *I like to wash my hair every day.*)
3 d – *Try doing* is more of a suggestion or an experiment (eg *I'll try phoning him, he might be in.*)
4 c – *Try to do* suggests effort or difficulty (eg *I tried to stop her, but she wouldn't listen.*)
5 f – If you stop doing something, you cease that activity, so you are now avoiding him.
6 e – If you stop to do something, that is why you have stopped.
7 g – *I remember telling him* means that I now have a memory of that event.
8 h – *I remembered to tell him*: the remembering is before the telling.

7 Students work individually to choose the most appropriate form. Check in pairs then as a class.

Answers

1 taking
2 organizing
3 to learn
4 to think
5 setting (or possibly *to set* if there is an idea of difficulty in this)
6 to do
7 to finish
8 starting
9 making

Refer students to the Grammar and vocabulary bank on page 157, where there is further practice of the *-ing* form and infinitive.

Vocabulary   page 109

Expressions to describe skills

Aim

The aim of this section is to expand learners' vocabulary to talk about the topic of learning. They can then use the vocabulary in the next speaking section, a model for which is given in the recording.

1 Students should work individually, or in pairs, to try and complete the expressions using the words from the boxes. Check as a class.

Answers

1 natural, practical	8 uptake
2 common	9 all rounder
3 aptitude	10 steep
4 quick	11 deep
5 highly	12 pick
6 high	13 step
7 good	

2 (O) **2.9** Students now listen to the recording and tick any of the words and phrases they hear Josie use.

Answers

1 She was not successful; she didn't have an aptitude for driving.
2 pick (it) up; quick learner; in at the deep end; have an aptitude for; steep learning curve

(O) **2.9**

I didn't learn to drive until I was about 25, which is pretty unusual in this country, I think. Most people learn as soon as they can, when they're 17. But I lived in London, where the public transport is pretty good, so I didn't really need a car.

[pause]

When I got a job where I needed to drive, I wasn't really worried about learning, I thought I would pick it up pretty easily. I'm usually a quick learner so I decided to book myself an intensive driving course. A lesson every day for two weeks and then I'd take the test. Talk about throwing yourself in at the deep end!

[pause]

Well, although I was so confident, it turned out I didn't really have an aptitude for driving. In fact, I was terrible. And I had to pass the test because my new job depended on it. It was certainly a steep learning curve! I didn't actually pass the first time. I think I was just too nervous, but I took the test again a week later, and this time I did pass!

Speaking   page 110

IELTS Speaking Part 2

1 Put the students in pairs. Students then look at the question on the card. They have one minute to think about what they are going to say and make notes if they wish.

2 They then take it in turns to talk about the question for two minutes. Monitor and take note of good vocabulary you hear being used. You could feedback to the class on this at the end, rather than focusing on errors this time.

IELTS Speaking Part 3

3 In pairs, or possibly small groups, students can then talk about the Part 3 type questions. The previous focus on vocabulary will hopefully encourage them to also use new words and expressions in this task.

Writing   pages 110–112

IELTS Writing Task 2: Organization and coherence: paragraphing

Aim

This section focuses on the structure and coherence of essays with particular attention given to paragraphing. Students build up an essay in a structured way, with plenty of guidance, before carrying out a parallel task on their own.

1 Students read the question and underline the key words before deciding what should be included in the essay.

Answers

key words: academic achievement, school, university, only true measure, intelligence
option a

2 Point out that the same question is being referred to and then ask students to work in pairs to read the introductions and judge which is the best and why the others are less suitable.

Answers

Introduction 1
• Too brief
• Rather simplistic: *you need to be clever to do this.*

Introduction 2
Virtually repeats the question word for word in the first sentence. This is a common feature of students' answers. Point out that they will not gain any marks for copying the question, so in effect it is a waste of time. The second sentence is a very general statement that could be a bit more focussed.

Introduction 3
• Clear opening sentence
• Paraphrasing of question (eg *judged* instead of *true measure*, educational success instead of *academic achievement*.)
• Well-expressed sentences – simple and clear, range of structures and use of a linking word (*However*)
• Introduces the idea that the writer is questioning the statement and will develop his/her ideas in the essay.
All these points are positive features of a strong introduction. Therefore this is clearly the best introduction.

3 Identify which words are used in the best introduction to paraphrase the question.

Answers

The question is paraphrased as follows:
academic achievement – educational success; measure – judged/assess

4 Students first look at the possible topic sentences for paragraphs 2 and 3 and then add their own ideas for supporting ideas and examples. They could then compare their ideas in pairs and one or two of the best examples could be shown to the class.

5 Students read a possible paragraph 4 (only possible, as their own ideas may have taken this off in a different direction) and answer questions on the lexical links in the text. The aim here is to review the earlier work on lexical links and allow students to see how this awareness can be related to their own writing, as well as helping them to follow a text when reading. Draw their attention to the relevant Tip.

Answers

1 A final example
2 They
3 learning about a subject independently
4 dealing with a variety of real-life situations and problems
5 such difficulties

6 Ask students how they think the essay will conclude. They should be able to tell that the author does not agree with the statement.

7 Students should write their own conclusion, in line with the arguments in the model they have been working with. Draw their attention to the Tip before they start. They can then compare what they have written with the model answer on page 163.

8 Students are now going to carry out the same sequence in a parallel task. Start by asking them to underline key words in the question, in the same way as before. This should become a habit before starting any essay.

Answers

key words: parents, family background, influence, teachers, young person's learning, academic achievement

9 To help students get some ideas, allow them to work in pairs to add their own ideas to the list of arguments in agreement and disagreement.

10 They should then decide on two to three main arguments they wish to include in their essay and think of any supporting ideas or examples.

11 Draw students' attention to the Useful language box, for introductions and conclusions and then ask them to write their essay. This may be done for homework, but there are some advantages to writing in class as you can monitor and see how they are progressing. When they have finished, ask them to check through their answer for any mistakes before comparing their answer with the model answer on page 163.

Extra activity

Put the following lines from the model essay for exercise 1 onto the board. A common spelling mistake has been introduced into each one. Ask students to correct them, then check the correct version in the model answer.

– There is no doubt that people are often judged in terms of there educational success.
– However, this is surely not the only way too assess intelligence.
– They have successfully learned a skill which definately requires intelligence.
– Musicians have the skills to perform complex peices of music.
– Such skills cannot neccessarily be learned on a course or from a book.
– They have become 'educated' by learning about a subject independantly.

Listening   page 112

IELTS Listening Section 3: Note completion

Aim

This is a typical Part 3 dialogue between a lecturer and a student on an academic subject. Students need to complete notes, which include a diagram

 2.10 Ensure students understand the phrase 'nature versus nurture'. As a lead in, briefly discuss which they think has a greater influence. Then ask students to read the notes they have to complete, and predict possible answers or word class, etc.

Answers

1	(just) born clever	6	reasons or evidence
2	influence them	7	bibliography
3	2,000 words	8	according to author
4	Environmental	9	handout
5	results might differ	10	next tutorial

 2.10

[DW = Dr Williams; S = Sian]

DW: Hello there, Sian.

S: Hello, Dr Williams – I'd like to talk to you about my assignment please.

DW: Fine. Come on in and have a seat. Have you started work on it yet?

S: Yes, I have – I've started doing some reading around and I've roughed out an outline of what I want to do, but I wanted to just check with you that I was going in the right direction.

DW: OK, good. So what have you decided to look at?

S: What really interests me is the idea of 'nature vs nurture' with regard to intelligence and looking at whether a child is just born clever, or whether their parents, teachers, friends – people like that influence them. Do you think that this is a suitable subject for me to focus on?

DW: Well, it's a big topic for a 2,000-word assignment. People have been debating that for years, and there's still no definitive answer.

S: Yes, I know. I've been researching in the library though and I've found several studies that have tried to compare the effects of genetic factors and environmental factors on children.

DW: Well, there's no shortage of literature on this subject, that's for sure!

S: Yes! And that's my main problem at the moment. For every study that shows that genetic potential is the most important factor, there's another to show the opposite!

DW: The best thing to do is to choose a selection of research that shows a similar pattern, and compare that in relation to one or two studies which don't follow the same trends. Then try to analyse why the results might differ.

S: OK. Another question I wanted to ask you was whether I should include my own opinion?

DW: It's fine to do that, but be careful not to make your writing sound too personal, that is, make sure that you back up any statements with clear reasons or evidence and don't forget to make reference to where you found that information.

S: What do you mean, exactly?

DW: Well, for example, if you say that in Australia fewer children from lower-income families go to university, even though that's a fairly well-known fact, you need to mention the source of that information.

S: You mean find a study that has shown that?

DW: Yes, and include the reference in your bibliography at the end of your assignment.

S: The bibliography – should that include all the books I've used for reference?

DW: No, only the ones that you've directly cited in the essay. Put them in alphabetical order according to author – not in the order that you use them in the essay. Remember: you were given a handout on this topic at the start of term.

S: Yes, that's right. Right – thanks for your time. I'll go and get on with it!

DW: OK – goodbye. If you have any further questions or points you want to discuss, then we can cover these in your next tutorial.

S: Great. Thank you for your help. Bye.

DW: Cheerio.

Hedging

Aim
This section aims to raise awareness of a key feature of academic style: hedging. An awareness of this can help students in a number of ways. When writing themselves, it can help them to adopt a more impersonal style and when carrying out reading tasks it can help them to answer questions about the writer's opinions more effectively.

1 Elicit the key difference from the students: that the first sentence is much more tentative. Establish how this is achieved: using impersonal or tentative phrases such as *Many people believe, it is often the case that …*

2 Look at the explanation together and then ask students to find further examples of hedging in the two sentences.

Answers
1 Sometimes, can have, possibly
2 It appears, may be

3 Students can then try to make a list of ways of hedging and compare their ideas with those listed in the Grammar and vocabulary bank on page 157.

4 Students should rewrite the sentences given, using some different hedging devices.

Possible answers
1 It could be said that teachers might have a particularly important role to play if the child lacks support from home, perhaps due to emotional or financial difficulties which could have a negative effect on their learning.
2 Many people believe that it is possible for a child to succeed academically, perhaps even without the help of a supportive family.

Idioms

Aim
This activity aims to further develop the students' awareness of collocations, this time looking at a set of collocates linked to the words *brain* and *mind*, which may be confused.

5 Ask students to complete the idioms, using their sense of what seems to collocate. They can then check their answers using a good dictionary, ideally a collocations dictionary.

Answers

1	brain	3	mind	5	mind
2	mind	4	brain	6	brain

Extra activity
Vocabulary recycling: A bluffing game with a dictionary
Ensure students have access to a good mono-lingual learner's dictionary in pairs. Ask them to look through and choose two words that they don't know, but which they think are useful. At this stage it is a good idea to monitor carefully to check that the words they have chosen are not too obscure. Now ask them to write down three definitions for each one (ie six definitions in total). Each word should have its correct definition, and two false, but plausible definitions (which they could find from the dictionary). You may need to model this process for them on the board.
Arrange the class into groups of four (two pairs together). Each pair should take it in turns to read their word and three definitions to the other pair, who try to guess the correct one. A point is gained for each word correctly identified. The word and the definition should be noted down.
When each pair has given their two words to the other pair, groups can be swapped around and the game played again. At the end, ensure each student has several new words complete with definitions to put in their vocabulary books.

Content overview

Themes

This unit looks at the theme of leisure from different angles: leisure activities and sports, technology and the internet and developing leisure trends.

Exam related activities

Reading

Multiple choice
Summary completion
Labelling a diagram

Writing

Task 2   Describing problems and solutions

Listening

Section 1   Form completion
Section 3   Short answer questions
            Sentence completion
            Matching

Speaking

Part 2   Describing leisure activities
Part 3   Discussing changes in leisure activities over time

Language development

Leisure activities
-ing form and infinitive to talk about likes and preferences
Expressions with future meaning
The internet

Skills development

Study skills

Using negative prefixes to work out meaning

Vocabulary   pages 114–115

Leisure activities

Aim

This section aims to provide students with a range of vocabulary to talk about their leisure pursuits and a set of adjectives to describe leisure pursuits. It also gives students some further practice in reading and understanding graphs.

Optional lead in

Tell students about some of your leisure interests. You should include one activity or interest which is not true. Ask the class to guess which is not true, based on what they know about you. Then ask them to carry out a similar task with a partner.

1   Ask students to look at the leisure activities in the box and put them in order, from those they do most often to those they do least often. They should then compare their answers in pairs or small groups.

2   Ask students to compare their answers with the results of the survey shown in the bar graph. Ask a few questions to the class as a whole to check understanding of the graph, eg *What percentage of men took part in sport or exercise? What was more popular with women, listening to music or reading?*

3   Elicit any differences they have noticed between men and women, eg *Men spend more time than women on sport/exercise, using the internet and playing computer games. Women spend more time than men with friends and family, reading, shopping and arts and crafts.* See if, from their previous answers, the same differences exist in the class.

4   Students should now look at the second graph. Check some of the potentially more difficult vocabulary: *conditioning activities, recreational, snooker, pool, billiards, pitch and putt, darts.* Then either discuss the questions in pairs or small groups, or as a class.

5   Ask students to match the equipment in the box to the activities in the second chart.

Answers

ball: outdoor football, snooker, pool, billiards
board: darts
club: golf, pitch and putt, putting
cue: snooker, pool, billiards
goggles: swimming or diving
helmet: cycling
table: snooker, pool, billiards
trainers: all except swimming and diving (but playing some sports to a high level requires special shoes)
weights: gym activities

6 Students now check if they have the vocabulary they need to describe their own sporting or physical activities. This is important to make sure that they are able to talk effectively about their hobbies in the Speaking test. It may be useful to take in some dictionaries or use an online dictionary for this stage.

7 Students work together to discuss which adjectives they would choose to describe any of the activities in the chart and why.

Listing   page 115

IELTS Listening Section 1: Form completion

1 Students should discuss the questions together.

Possible answers

keep fit classes, weight training, gym activities, swimming
(in a larger gym there may be a hall for badminton, softball, etc.)

2 Ask students to look at the form before they listen and try to predict what kind of answers they are looking for. For example, question 1 is going to be a number (Julie's age).

3 (O) 2.11 Students listen and complete the form. Depending on the level of the class, you may let them listen again to check their answers, but make sure that they realize that in the exam they will only hear it once.

Note that there is a pause on the recording after *That's one of the reasons I felt I needed to join the gym.*

Answers

1 24	5 weight	8 Wednesday
2 9	6 aerobic	9 6.00
3 10,000	7 twice a week	10 Siobhan
4 sitting down		

(O) 2.11

[I = Instructor; J = Julie]

I: Welcome to Fitness Fanatics Health Club. I'd just like to start by taking a few personal details, if I may. Your full name is ...?

J: Julie Ann Edmonson.

I: Thank you, and you're 23, Julie, is that right?

J: Yes, oh actually, no, <u>24</u>. It was my birthday last week.

I: And can I have a contact telephone number, please?

J: Yes, it's 0798 674 5689.

I: And what's the best time to contact you?

J: Oh, after work would be better really. Any time between, say 6 and <u>9pm</u>.

I: Fine. Now in a little while, we'll do some fitness tests and I'll ask you a bit more about your medical history, but first of all, I'd like to know a little more about why you've decided to join the gym. What kind of exercise do you do at the moment?

J: Well, I do quite a bit of walking. I bought myself a pedometer last year and I'm trying to do at least <u>10,000</u> steps a day. I don't always make it though!

I: That's great. Walking's a good start. And do you get much exercise at work?

J: No, not really. It's pretty much a desk job you see, there's a lot of <u>sitting down</u>. That's one of the reasons I felt I needed to join the gym.
[pause]

I: Yes, so what specific benefits are you looking for from joining the gym? For example, would you like to lose weight, or just get fitter?

J: I'm quite happy with my weight, but I'd like to keep it this way.

I: Uh huh, <u>weight maintenance</u> then. Anything else? Fitness goals?

J: Yes, although I'm doing the walking, it doesn't leave me out of breath, you know. I don't feel that I really get a lot of <u>aerobic exercise</u> – so I'd like to increase that.

I: Yes, that's fine. I think there are a number of ways we could help you achieve your targets. How many times a week were you thinking of coming, and for how long?

J: Er, well, I know I should come three times a week, but, if I'm honest it's only going to be <u>twice a week</u>, for about an hour or so.

I: Are you interested in doing any classes, or would you rather just use the gym?

J: I'm not sure, what classes do you have?

I: Oh, quite a range. We have a new class that's very popular, Zumba. That's all about getting a workout by dancing to Latin music. It's on a <u>Wednesday</u> night at 6.30.

J: That sounds interesting, but I'm not great at dancing, really, I prefer swimming. Do you have any aqua aerobics classes?

I: Yes, we do. On a Thursday evening at <u>6.00pm</u>. Shall I put you down for that?

J: Yes, I'll give it a try. And what about the gym? Will someone show me round?

I: Yes, we'll need to make an appointment with one of our fitness instructors. Could you come tomorrow evening?

J: Er, I could, but I'd rather come on Friday if that's possible? Any time after 7.00pm.

I: OK, then, you have an appointment at 7.00 with Mark.

J: Oh, I think I'd prefer to have a female trainer actually.

I: No problem, <u>Siobhan</u> is free at 7pm as well.

J: Could you spell that please?

I: S-I-O-B-H-A-N.

J: Thanks, that's great.

Expressing preferences

Aim
Students will frequently need to talk about likes and preferences, but the verb patterns used with these common verbs can be confusing. This section should help to clarify the rules.

1 Ask students to look at the extracts and choose the correct form. If you monitor at this stage you should be able to get some idea of how well they already understand the language point. Students can then listen to the previous recording again to check their answers.

Answers

1	to lose	3	use	5	come
2	to keep	4	swimming	6	to have

2 Students can then look at the Grammar and vocabulary bank and/or you can explain the rules before they complete the sentences with the correct verb form.

Note that there is further practice in the Grammar and vocabulary bank on page 157 as well, which could be done for consolidation or homework.

Answers

1	watching, listening	4	do
2	to play, play	5	to go
3	to stay	6	say

Reading   pages 116–118

Aim
The reading in this section provides practice of three exam question types: multiple choice with three answers, summary completion and labelling a diagram.

1 Draw students' attention to the first sentence of the reading text and ask them to discuss the questions, either in pairs, small groups or as a class.

2 Students now read the full text and decide if the writer agrees with Keynes' predictions. This stage is designed to give them an overview of the text and should be carried out fairly quickly. You may like to set a time limit of 3 to 4 minutes.

Answer
The writer does not agree; the number of hours people work is rising, but so is the amount of leisure time.

3 Multiple choice

Exam information
In the previous unit students had a multiple choice question where they had to choose two options. In this question, they need to choose three. Take the opportunity to remind students to always read the rubric carefully.

Questions 1–3
Students should look at the options and see which ones can be found in the text. Remind students that the information is likely to be paraphrased, and encourage them to underline the sections in the text where they found the answers.

Answers

A – *… we do in fact have a little more leisure time than 40 years ago, as a result of washing machines, online grocery shopping and so on.*

C – *… the number of hours people work is likely to continue rising, with more European countries following the American model of a longer working week and few holidays.*

D – *… we will be expected to work on the train on the way to work, at home while we prepare an evening meal and even in bed.*

Summary completion

Questions 4–9

Exam information
Students have previously completed a summary (in Unit 8), but this is the other version of the task, where words are provided to choose from.

Encourage students to look at the summary as a whole and try to guess which part of speech they are likely to need. This should help them to narrow down their options. They then try to complete the summary using the words in the box.

Answers

4	L (reducing)	7	D (fuel)
5	B (activities)	8	A (family)
6	O (longer)	9	F (cultural)

Labelling a diagram

Questions 10–14
Students now label the diagrams on page 117, using no more than TWO words from the text.

Answers

10	experiences	13	clothing
11	material goods	14	1986
12	self-actualization		

Language focus   pages 118–119

Expressions with future meaning

Aim

In this section, students look at some different expressions which can be used to talk about the future. These should be useful for both the speaking and writing parts of IELTS.

1 Draw students' attention to the different ways of expressing the future, then ask them to find further examples in the reading text.

Answers

1 aim to provide, expected to work, hope to achieve anticipate a further growth, predict this pattern continuing (*note that these expressions are quite formal*)
2 may spend, may be, could reverse
3 is likely to

2 If students need further more controlled practice, refer them to the Grammar and vocabulary bank on page 158. Otherwise, ask students to rewrite the predictions according to how likely each of them thinks that they are. Obviously answers will vary for this task, as it is personalized.

Possible answers

1 In the future we are likely to have more leisure time.
2 Within a few years I expect we will do all our shopping online.
3 By the end of the century I predict that people will be living on another planet.
4 In a few years' time we're sure to pay for everything by mobile phone.

Vocabulary   pages 119–120

The internet

Aim

In this section students will expand their vocabulary for talking about the internet. They will probably already have some vocabulary, so the word map format will enable them to activate this. It is also a useful way to record vocabulary in a lexical set, which they could use again. The discussion questions at the end of the section should allow them to use some of the vocabulary and also act as a lead in to the listening task that follows.

1 Look at the word map together and check students understand how it works by doing one or two words from the box as an example. Then ask them to complete the word map.

Answers

Places you can visit: blog, social networking site, webpage
Equipment: laptop, mouse, screen, smartphone, tablet
Communication: chatting, instant messaging (IM), texting

2 Now ask students to work together to add any other words and phrases they might know. Monitor and check their ideas and then share some of the words and phrases as a class.

Possible answers

Places you can visit: website
Equipment: software, ISP (internet service provider)
Communication: skype
Other: download, upload, shop, play games

3 Ask students to answer the questions individually. There are no correct answers, so students should simply try to answer honestly.

4 Students then compare their answers in pairs or small groups and discuss their beliefs and attitudes about the idea of internet addiction.

Listening   page 120

IELTS Listening Section 3

Aim

In this section students will listen to two students talking in a seminar, a typical Section 3 context. The task types practised are short answer questions, sentence completion and matching.

Exam information

Matching may be a new task type for the students. Encourage them to look through all the opinions first and remind them that what they hear on the recording is likely to be a paraphrase rather than a word-for-word reflection. They should also be clear that each person expresses only ONE of the opinions shown.

Short answer questions, Sentence completion and Matching

Questions 1–3, Questions 4–7 and Questions 8–10

1 (O) **2.12 and 2.13** Look at the rubric explaining the situation and ask students to look through the questions first. Using the Tip, remind students that they should not change the grammatical form of the word from what they hear on the recording.

Answers

1	26%	6	concentration
2	eight	7	checking
3	1–2	8	E
4	junk	9	B
5	growth	10	A

 2.12

[T =Tutor; R = Rob; J = Julie]

T: So, Rob, you've been looking at the topic of internet addiction. How's your research going so far?

R: Well, I started off by looking at some research done by Cranfield University School of Management. They carried out a survey of 260 secondary school pupils and the results were quite interesting – a bit worrying, actually. They found that 26% of those surveyed spent more than six hours on the web a day.

J: That's incredible. Six hours?

R: More than six hours, actually. Sixty-three per cent of them felt that they were addicted to the internet and 53% felt that they couldn't live without their mobile phones. Interestingly, 62% of them were bought their first computer around the age of eight. So maybe it's down to their parents if they're addicted now. Most of them also had a mobile phone between the ages of eight and ten and started using a social networking site at the age of eleven. On average, they now spend one to two hours a day on social network sites like Facebook.

T: But is it necessarily a bad thing to be online a lot?

R: Well, there are the physical issues for a start. If you spend that much time online, you tend to get less exercise and have a poor diet. You just eat junk food in front of the screen. And if you're staying up late, you're probably not getting enough sleep, which can affect your growth as a teenager. Teenagers need more sleep, not less. You are probably consuming more caffeine as well, which can lead to poor concentration. You could also develop repetitive strain injury from typing on a keyboard, clicking a mouse or texting and there was a recent case where someone had an accident on the motorway because she kept checking a social networking website page while she was driving along!

 2.13

[T =Tutor; R = Rob; J = Julie]

J: But surely these are all extreme cases. I mean most people wouldn't be so stupid as to be going online while trying to drive, would they?

R: No, I think that is pretty extreme. But I think being online for six or more hours a day is quite extreme too, and the research showed that this is pretty normal for those teenagers.

J: I think it depends what they're doing. If they're just playing games, then I guess that's a bit of a waste of time. But a lot of students use the internet to research stuff, don't they? There's a lot of useful information out there.

T: Yes, I think that's a good point. But I think they need to know how to navigate the web successfully. There's a lot of rubbish out there too and it's no good if students think that research just means going to a site like Wikipedia, where the information isn't properly checked.

J: And I don't think there's anything wrong with social networking is there? It's just the same as chatting to friends on the phone or even face to face. Isn't it a good thing that we have more choices now? We can use email, or instant messaging or Twitter.

R: I don't think it is just the same thing, actually. A lot of people have 'friends' online that they've never met. How can that be a proper friendship? I think it's damaging people's ability to socialize actually, and it's definitely damaging people's ability to write properly, all these abbreviations that people use when they're texting. I read somewhere that students are starting to use them in essays now. How can that be a positive thing?

2 Students now have a chance to respond to the recording by discussing their opinions about the statements in exercise 1.

3 To provide an opportunity to recycle the vocabulary from the previous section, students listen again and note down which of the computer- or internet-related words they hear.

Answers

Track 2.12: internet, computer, social networking site, online, screen, keyboard, mouse, texting
Track 2.13: online, internet, navigate, chatting, instant messaging, Twitter, texting

Speaking page 121

IELTS Speaking Part 2

Aim

This section gives students an opportunity to use some of the ideas and vocabulary from the unit to practice parts 2 and 3 of the speaking test. In addition, they will listen to a model answer and develop their speaking skills by learning some different phrases to support their answers with examples.

1 **2.14** Students should start by looking at the two speaking cards. They then listen to the recording and make a note about Ravi's key points. Make sure that students can see the connection between what he says and the key points on card A.

Answers

favourite activity: walking
how often: tries to do it every day, sometimes for whole day
equipment: trainers, map, food and drink
enjoys it because it's good for having ideas and good exercise

 2.14

Well, probably my favourite thing to do in my free time is walking. I particularly like walking in the countryside or the mountains, you know, taking the whole day. But I do try to do some walking just about every day. Sometimes I go on my own, and sometimes with friends.

I don't need much equipment, really. Just a good pair of trainers or walking boots if I'm going a bit further, a map maybe, something to eat and drink. Oh, and if I'm on my own I take my MP3 player and listen to some music while I walk.

I find it really relaxing. Often when I start walking my mind is absolutely full of thoughts, but as I walk they just start to go away and I get more and more relaxed. And I have some of my best ideas when I'm walking too. And, of course, it's good for you, definitely good exercise.

2 Students then work in pairs and choose one question each to prepare and talk about, as in the IELTS Speaking test. Monitor and perhaps note down errors and/or good examples of language for class feedback.

3 When students have finished, ask them to discuss the question given.

IELTS Speaking Part 3

4 Ask students to look at the different ways of giving an example. Remind them that having a variety of ways of saying the same thing will improve the perceived level of their spoken English. Students then listen to Ravi speaking on the same topic they have just discussed, and note which phrases he uses.

Answers

take, for example, for instance

(O)2.15

[E = Examiner; R = Ravi]
E: Do you think that people have more or less time for leisure now than in the past?
R: Oh, I think people have less time, definitely. Everyone works so hard these days, don't they? Take email for example. Now everyone expects you to reply to emails even in the evenings or at weekends. That's got to affect how much time you have for leisure. For instance, I work 9 to 5 in the office, but I always spend another hour looking at emails when I get home.

5 Establish the importance of giving examples to back up what you are saying, before giving students the opportunity to discuss the further questions related to the theme of leisure.

Writing   pages 122–124

IELTS Writing Task 2

Aim

This Writing Task 2 is an example of a 'problem-solution' type essay. This kind of essay starts by identifying a problem (or problems) and then sets out one or more solutions. In this section, students will be shown exactly how to plan and structure an essay of this type, exploring a model before they write their own.

1 As with previous writing tasks, students should underline the key words in the question. This will help them to focus on the key points they need to address.

Possible answers

key words: cyberbullying, new technologies, internet, mobile phones, bully and harass young people, increase, causes, effects, solutions, individuals, schools

2 Ask students to read the sample essay and identify the main idea in each paragraph. This should enable them to see that the essay follows the order suggested in the question: first dealing with causes, then effects and finally solutions.

Answers

the causes – paragraph 1
the effects – paragraph 2
possible solutions for individuals – paragraph 3
possible solutions for schools – paragraph 3

3 Students now start to look more closely at the problems and solutions described in the essay. Ask them to read the essay again and list the problems and solutions they can find. Problems should be divided into cause and effect.

Answers

Problems	Solutions
Causes: access to internet and smartphones which enable cyberbullies to spread photos, gossip, etc. around very quickly to lots of people Effects: embarrassment needing psychiatric help	Individuals should not respond to the bully. Tell someone. Schools should have anti-bullying policies. Students should be aware of the policy and the punishment for bullying. Schools should deal strictly with bullying.

4 Now draw students' attention to the Useful language box and again ask them to find examples in the sample essay. This will help them to see how the phrases can be used in context.

Answers

..., it has also <u>led to</u> a growth in cyberbullying.

... the embarrassment that <u>resulted from</u> this <u>caused</u> the boy to need psychiatric help.

5 To ensure that students are able to use the phrases correctly, ask them to rewrite the sentences, using the stems given and a suitable cause or result word or phrase. Note that the phrases using a dependent preposition (*result in/lead to*) are followed by an *-ing* form.

Answers

1 The growth in mobile technology has caused more cyber-bullying.
  The growth in mobile technology has resulted in more cyber-bullying.
2 As a consequence of the embarrassment, the boy needed psychiatric help.
  The boy needed psychiatric help because of/as a consequence of/as a result of the embarrassment.
  As a result of the embarrassment, the boy needed psychiatric help.
3 The embarrassment resulted in the boy needing psychiatric help.
  The embarrassment led to the boy needing psychiatric help.

6 Students now look at another problem-solution type essay. Ask them to underline the key words as before (*young people, so much time, affecting their health, causes, effects, possible solutions*). They should see that the essay can be structured in a very similar way to the sample they studied earlier. Working in pairs, students can then brainstorm problems (causes and effects) and solutions.

7 Students can then use the framework given, which mirrors the earlier example, to write a plan for their own essay. Point out to them that, even given the limited time available in the IELTS test, they should spend a few minutes like this thinking of ideas and making a rough plan.

8 Students write a first draft of their essay. At this stage in the course, you may like to get them to write it in class, with a time limit similar to that in the exam (about 40 minutes, including planning time).

9 On page 124 there is a sample answer. It would probably be better not to let the students look at this until they have written their own version. Once they have completed their version, they can look at the sample and underline causes, effects and solutions.

Answers

Causes: increased access to the internet; time spent on the web socializing on social networking sites; parents preferring to supervise children at home instead of letting them play unsupervised (paragraph 2)
Effects: children are not getting enough exercise; obesity, diabetes and other health problems (paragraph 3)
Solutions: parents and schools should encourage young people to take enough exercise; youth groups should be set up where young people can socialize and exercise (paragraph 4)

10 Students can then compare their own answer with the sample given. Encourage them to pick out useful phrases that they could include in their own work, such as *Probably the largest factor is ...* or *... have a responsibility to ...* and make any changes to the structure or language of their own essay.

Refer students to the Grammar and vocabulary bank on page 158, where there is further practice of using language to describe cause and effect.

Study skills page 125

Negative prefixes

1 Use this question to elicit that certain prefixes carry a negative meaning. Point out to students that prefixes often carry a specific meaning, which can be very useful when trying to guess what a word means.

Answer

They have the negative prefixes *im-, in-* and *un-*.

2 Students write the prefixes then think of examples for them. Tell them to watch out for words which begin with these letters but not the actual prefix (eg *important* doesn't mean *not 'portant'*).

Possible answers

dis-	not, or to reverse an action	discontinue
re-	again or back	redo, reverse
trans-	across	transatlantic
anti-	against	anticlockwise
mis-	wrong or badly	misadventure
il-	not (with some words beginning with *l*)	illegal
pre-	before	pre-cooked
micro-	small	microchip

3 Working in pairs or small groups, ask students to try and guess the meanings of each prefix. If they find this difficult you could give them examples that might help: *monolingual, unique, binoculars, triangle, quarter, decimal.* Also mention that *cent* means 100, *kilo* means 1,000 *milli* can mean 1,000 (eg *a million*) or more often $\frac{1}{1000}$ (eg *a millimetre, a milligram*).

Answers

1 uni-	3 tri-	10 dec-
2 bi-	4 quadri-	

4 Ask students to complete the sentences using the adjectives given plus an appropriate prefix.

Answers

1 dishonest	4 impolite
2 irrelevant	5 immoral
3 misbehave	6 uncertain

5 Students should be able to make a good guess at the meanings of the words by looking at the prefix. They can check their answers in a dictionary and see at the same time how many other words begin the same way.

Answers

1 a bicycle with a single wheel
2 to manage something badly
3 the science that deals with very small living things
4 a railway system in which trains travel on a single track
5 something which is already wrapped or in a box when you buy it
6 across several national borders
7 consisting only of the colours black, white and grey (one colour in effect)
8 a type of film on which pictures and writing can be made very small
9 form a wrong opinion about a person or situation
10 a small vehicle, like a motorbike, but with four wheels

Extra activity
Vocabulary recycling: Using word maps
Having done the word map exercises on page 119, you could encourage students to review vocabulary from a previous unit, using this method. Choose a lexical set of words from a previous unit, eg from Unit 8, related to health and medicine. Give pairs of students large pieces of paper and ask them to put these words into a mind map, and then use their dictionaries to look up and add other vocabulary to the map. These could be displayed around the classroom.

11 The art of advertising

Content overview

Themes
This unit focuses on the theme of advertising and features global marketing and newer forms of advertising such as stealth and guerilla marketing.

Exam related activities

Reading
Matching headings to paragraphs
Note completion
Multiple choice
Sentence completion (with choices)

Writing
Task 2   Presenting a balanced argument

Listening
Section 3   Classification and table completion

Speaking
Part 2   A memorable advertisement
Part 3   Advertising and brands

Language development

Language focus and Vocabulary
Modals of obligation and prohibition
Formal and academic language
Advertising and marketing

Skills development

Reading skills
Identification of beliefs or arguments

Study skills
Understanding verbs in essay titles

Collocations
Synonyms which collocate differently: *a major problem, a fundamental right*.

Reading   pages 126–128

Aim
In this section, students read a text taken from an academic textbook. This is quite typical of IELTS, but may be a little harder than some of the texts tackled previously, as it is of more specific, rather than general, interest.

1 Ask students to look at the wordle. Explain that a wordle is a way of looking at a text and seeing which words are used most frequently in a visual way; these words are larger. Ask students to identify the biggest words in the wordle. Explain any unknown words (particularly the larger words, as these are highest frequency in the text) or ask them to use their dictionaries. Some key words to deal with might be: *global, brand, product, market* (noun and verb), *standardization, influential*. Then ask students to discuss why *different* is the biggest word (because the text is about cultural differences).

2 If you think students could still benefit from the support, you could ask them to skim the text first and check their predictions. Otherwise, you could ask them to go straight into answering the questions, as they would in the exam.

Matching headings to paragraphs

Questions 1–7
Students should be quite familiar with this task type by now. Remind students not to simply word match, but to read the whole paragraph. For example, paragraph C begins with a discussion of Coca Cola®, which may lead students to choose heading i. However, the paragraph as a whole is not about launching a soft drink product but about adapting products for different markets (heading ix).

Answers

1 vii	2 ix	3 v	4 ii	5 viii	6 iii	7 x

Note completion

Questions 8–11
Encourage students to read through the notes first

and consider what type of answer they are looking for. For example, question 8 is looking for a verb which describes something businesses now have a chance to do globally, question 9 is likely to be the name of a company and so on.

Answers

8	broaden their markets	10	'Sprinkler'
9	Nissan	11	Hollywood

Multiple choice

Questions 12–13
Give the students a chance to look through the multiple choice questions first and identify where in the text the answer is likely to be found. Point out that the word *concludes* in question 13 is a good indication that this answer will be found towards the end of the text.

Answers

12 C   13 B

Vocabulary   page 129

Formal and academic language

Look at the first question together with students to illustrate how *determine* is a lower frequency and more formal way of saying *decide*. Students are unlikely to know the more formal words and phrases highlighted in this section, but doing this exercise should help them to see how they may be able to work out the meaning of unknown words and phrases, as well as increasing their awareness of more formal language.

Answers

1 determine
2 promoting
3 as is evident
4 to make its appeal as broad as possible
5 simultaneously
6 prior to
7 grave
8 attempting to broaden its operations globally
9 the most viable option

Speaking   page 129

Aim
In this section, students learn a useful set of vocabulary related to the topic of advertising and marketing and then use the lexis to carry out a Part 2 and Part 3 Speaking test.

1 Ask students to try and match the words to the definitions. Then check as a class and clarify any difficulties. Check students are able to pronounce the words (especially *logo* and *slogan*) as they will need them for the speaking activities.

Answers

1 C   2 A   3 D   4 F   5 B   6 G   7 E

IELTS Speaking Part 2

2 Give students a few minutes to look at the question and consider what they could say, and what vocabulary they might use. Then ask them to take turns in pairs to talk about the subject on the card.

IELTS Speaking Part 3

3 In the same pairs, students take it in turns to answer the pairs of questions. At this stage in the course, students should be familiar with the exam format and what is expected, so you could ask them to give each other feedback on their answers. For example, did they use a good range of language, did they speak at sufficient length?

The photocopiable activity for this unit is also related to the topic of advertising.

Reading   pages 130–132

Aim
This text presents two different sets of opinions and is a good opportunity for students to develop their ability to identify the claims of the writer(s), using the task type Yes, No, Not Given, rather than the similar True, False, Not given.

1 Ask students to look at the cartoons and say how the people are trying to encourage or persuade others to buy something.

Answers

In the first cartoon the man in the boat is causing the people on the ship to need the rubber rings. In the second the man is using the situation to make a recommendation.

2 Students read the two definitions and discuss which type of marketing the cartoons might represent. Ask them what their opinion of this type of marketing is.

Answers

The first could be seen as guerilla marketing as it is imaginative, but guerilla marketing is usually more about entertaining people than drowning them! The second is stealth marketing as the cold man thinks the other man is just being helpful.

3 Ask students to quickly read the text and find any examples of stealth or guerrilla marketing.

Note that there is further practice of phrasal verbs related to the text in the Grammar and vocabulary bank on page 159. This could be done before the exam-related work, afterwards, or as follow-up homework.

Answers

stealth marketing: company products marketed using teenagers

guerrilla marketing: mobile phones in 2002; dog food on the underground

4 Yes, No, Not given and Sentence completion

Questions 1–5, Questions 6–9 and Questions 10–13
Ask students to work through the exam style questions on the text. The task types covered are Yes, No, Not given and sentence completion. With the first two sets of questions, encourage students to underline the claims they find in the text related to each answer.

Answers

1	N (other way around)	8	NG
2	N (they are made to)	9	N (can be just as sneaky)
3	Y	10	C
4	NG	11	F
5	Y	12	D
6	Y	13	A
7	Y		

5 Ask students to discuss which of the opinions they most agree with, and say why. This will help to prepare them for the later writing task.

Language focus   pages 132–133

Modals of obligation and prohibition

Aim
Here students look at some contextualised examples of modal verbs of obligation and prohibition (from the reading text) and explore their meaning and form, as well as some other useful verbs with similar meanings. These verbs are all frequently used in IELTS writing tasks, and thus this section is linked to the next, on writing.

1 Draw students' attention to the sentences from the reading text on page 131, which all contain examples of modal verbs. In order to check students' understanding of the meaning of these modals of obligation and prohibition, ask them to put the modals shown into the correct categories.

Answers

Obligation			Prohibition	
strong	weak	lack of obligation	strong	weak
must have to	*should needs to*	*didn't have to don't need to*	*mustn't*	*shouldn't*

2 Use the questions given to check students' awareness of form. You could also refer students to the Grammar and vocabulary bank on page 158.

Answers

must and *should*: bare infinitive
need and *have*: full infinitive with *to*

3 Students write the modals in the past. This is a complicated area, as choosing the wrong past form can alter the meaning. Check understanding carefully.

Answers

Present time	Past time
should	*should have* + past participle
have to	*had to* + infinitive
must	*had to* + infinitive
mustn't	*was/weren't allowed to* + infinitive
need	*needed* + infinitive
don't need to	*didn't need to/needn't have* + past participle
don't have to	*didn't have to* + infinitive
shouldn't	*shouldn't have* + past participle

4 Ask students individually to complete the sentences. Monitor to ensure they are using appropriate modal verbs in the correct tense.

Answers

1	should have worked	4	had to work
2	have to wear	5	didn't need to bring
3	mustn't use		

5 This exercise presents other useful language for students in talking about obligation and prohibition. Look at the examples, and then ask students to write down five rules for their country, using the verbs. In multilingual classes, you could ask them to compare the rules in their different countries.

6 (○)**2.16** Depending on your students' listening skills, play the listening twice. Ask them to listen the first time for what was good or could be improved in the student's work. Then ask them to listen and write down the examples they hear of language of obligation/lack of obligation or prohibition.

Answers

good: ideas
needs improvement: too long, needed more examples, should compare and contrast, poor handwriting

Obligation	had to do, should have read, ought to have given, were supposed to compare
Lack of obligation	didn't need to word process
Prohibition	you mustn't do more than that, we aren't allowed to accept

 2.16

[S = Student; T = Tutor]

S: Can you explain what the problem was with my assignment on advertising standards?

T: Well, to begin with, it was much too long. We can accept up to 10% over the word limit, but <u>you mustn't do more than that</u>. We <u>aren't allowed</u> to accept an assignment of that length.

S: Oh, OK. I didn't realize that.

T: Then you really <u>should have read</u> the question more carefully. The question asked you to compare and contrast the rules applied by advertising standards agencies around the world and you only wrote about your own country.

S: So, I <u>ought to have given</u> more examples?

T: Yes, and you were also <u>supposed to</u> compare and contrast them, or say how they're different or similar.

S: Oh, I didn't understand that I <u>had to do</u> that. OK. Was that the only problem?

T: I'm afraid your handwriting wasn't very good either. You <u>didn't need to</u> word-process it, but it would have helped me to understand what you wanted to say. Having said all that, you did have some very good ideas about …

Optional activity

If appropriate, you could ask students to discuss how they think life at university will be different from their current lives, eg *I'll have to work even harder./I won't need to study so many subjects.*

Refer students to the Grammar and vocabulary bank on page 158, where there is further practice of modals of obligation and prohibition.

Writing   page 134

IELTS Writing Task 2

Aims

In this section, students look at a Task 2 type question which asks them to present two contrasting views before giving their own opinion, focusing on the structure of such an essay and how to present a balanced argument.

As a lead in to the writing task, students could discuss the ways different products are advertised in their own countries. If some students are unfamiliar with the lexical items *unethical* and *unacceptable*, elicit whether they are positive or negative and encourage them to guess the general meaning (medical ethics were discussed in Unit 8 so they should be able to do this).

Arguments for and against a viewpoint

1 Focus on the Task 2 question and underline the key words in the usual way. Point out how the key words indicate what students should be writing about, eg newer methods of advertising, not more traditional methods, whether these are unethical and/or unacceptable, and arguments from those who think this attitude is an over-reaction.

Answers

key words: newer methods, advertising, unethical, unacceptable in today's society, this viewpoint, over-reaction

2 Using the reading text on page 131, plus their own ideas, students make a list of arguments on both sides.

Answers

Unethical and unacceptable:
Advertisers should make it clear that the text is an advertisement.
Some famous advertising campaigns involved actors pretending to be tourists and then discussing the product with the public, which was dishonest.
Others used teenagers to promote the product and asked them not to admit that they were advertising the product. This is deception and should not be allowed.
The Government should control dishonest advertising practices by law.

Over-reaction:
The term 'buzz marketing' is more accurate as it is neither positive nor negative.
Advertising agencies are having to invent new ways of promoting their products.
One recent guerrilla marketing campaign involved actors dressing as dogs to promote dog food.
This was good fun, not deception.
Traditional advertising is old-fashioned and no longer works well.
Good advertising is very effective and gets the product talked about.
Another effective form of advertising is word of mouth, because people like to have products recommended by friends.
Modern advertising methods are no more manipulative than traditional advertising.
The Government should not be involved in controlling advertising.

3 Students have previously focused on impersonal statements in Unit 8, so this exercise should act as revision. Ask students to take some of the arguments from the previous exercise and make them impersonal, using the phrases given. Compare some examples as a class and make sure that students are clear that this is a good way of including opinions in an essay which they do not necessarily agree with themselves.

Example answers

It is sometimes thought that traditional advertising is old-fashioned.

It is widely believed that word of mouth is an effective form of advertising.

Many people find that a good advertising campaign is entertaining.

Perhaps the majority of people would agree that 'advertorials' are infuriating.

Those who feel bored by traditional advertising might argue that 'buzz' marketing creates interest.

4 Look at the Strategy box as a class. This is obviously not the only possible way of structuring such an essay, but it is a simple way of organizing it which students can use effectively.

Then ask students which of the words and phrases given could be used to start each paragraph. This should also check that they fully understand the purpose of each paragraph.

Possible answers

Paragraph 1 Over the last few years; In recent years
Paragraph 2 On the one hand; However; Having said that
Paragraph 3 On the other hand; However; Having said that
Paragraph 4 In my view; Personally; On balance, I would say that

5 Students can then use their ideas and outline plan to write the first draft of their essay. This would be a good opportunity to write under exam conditions in class, with a time limit of 40 minutes.

6 When they have written their draft, students can compare their work with the model answer given. You could ask students to answer the following questions about both the model and their own answer.

1 Does the essay follow the structure given?

2 Does it present a balanced argument for both sides?

3 Does it use appropriate phrases for beginning each paragraph? Underline them.

4 Does it use a range of vocabulary around the topic area? Underline the related words you can see.

5 Is the length appropriate?

7 Finally, ask students to write an answer to the second question given, using the same structure. This could be done for homework, but bear in mind that there is a model answer in the back of the book.

Students can compare their answer with the model answer on page 164 when they have finished, in the same way as suggested above.

Listening   page 136

IELTS Listening Section 3

Aim
In the following section, students will practise a Section 3 type listening, where three students are discussing an academic task. The question types covered are Classification and Table completion. After listening, students will use the information from the listening to carry out a speaking task, culminating in a short presentation.

1 Look at the diagram, showing the four Ps of the marketing mix, and ask students to consider what might be involved in each of these.

In order not to pre-empt the listening too much, it might be better to avoid a long discussion about the four Ps at this stage. However, after the listening, if any students are studying marketing, you could ask them to explain what these four elements involve or use the explanations below:

'The four Ps' is a term which has been used in marketing since the 1960s.

Product: this is what is being sold. It may be something tangible, such as a car, or a service.

Price: How much the product is being sold for. This needs to be considered carefully, comparing the product with other similar products and considering who is likely to buy the product and how much they may be willing or able to pay.

Promotion: This covers advertising, marketing, salesmanship and word of mouth.

Place: Where (and how) the product is to be sold (online, in particular stores, and so on).

2 Classification and Table completion

Questions 1–4 and Questions 5–10
(○) 2.17 and 2.18 Look at the first classification task and check students remember what to do (this task type was previously covered in Unit 3). One of the letters A, B, C will be used more than once.

Then look at the table and encourage students to use their predictions about the four Ps to guess what might go in these gaps.

Play the recording. Note that the section relating to questions 1–4 and that which relates to the table are on different tracks.

Answers

1	B	6	key features
2	C	7	product
3	C	8	competitive
4	A	9	to individuals/online
5	(an) (actual) item	10	communicating with

(○) 2.17

[K = Kate; T = Tom; I = Isabelle]

K: So, I think we should try and make some decisions about the presentation we're doing next week. Do you think we should talk for a third of the time each, or divide it up some other way?

T: I think we should probably divide it up by topic, rather than time. Isabelle?

I: Yes, I think that makes more sense.

K: OK, agreed.

T: We have 20 minutes, but don't forget we need to leave five minutes for questions at the end, so it's only 15 minutes for the talk itself.

K: Good point. Well, the obvious way to divide it is to have four sections, for the four parts of the marketing mix. You know, product, price, place and promotion ...

I: Sure. Shall we start with product? I'm happy to do that.

K: Yeah, that's fine.

T: <u>Actually, would you mind if I did that section?</u> That's the one I feel most confident about.

I: Oh, OK. No problem. Shall I look at promotion then?

K: That depends if you want to follow on from Tom. I think the next areas to look at would be price and place.

I: Yes, you're probably right. <u>How about if I do those then and you finish up with promotion.</u>

K: Fine.

T: OK, but we still need to look at the main points we're making, to make sure that what we're saying doesn't overlap.

(○) 2.18

[K = Kate; T = Tom; I = Isabelle]

I: OK, so what about if we go through each section and try and identify the main points?

T: Yes, good idea.

I: What are the main points we want to make about the product?

K: Well, it's important to say that a product can be either <u>an actual item</u> or a service.

T: Yes. Perhaps we could give some examples of different products at this point?

I: Good idea. That would help us with getting across the other key things to think about. For example, the design of a product and what its <u>key features</u> are.

K: And the brand name.

T: Yes, that's important. And the packaging too, if it's a product rather than a service.

K: Well, you can package a service too, can't you?

T: Well, I guess so, in a way.

I: OK, shall we move onto price? This very much <u>depends on the product</u>, doesn't it?

K: Yes, and the target market of course. In fact, I think the target market is very important. If it's aimed at people with money, they may well pay more regardless of whether the quality is really that high.

T: Mmm. Though quality is important, isn't it? <u>It's important to be competitive in your pricing.</u> If what you're selling is more expensive than the competition and not any better a product then you can't expect people not to notice, no matter how good your marketing is ...

K: I think that brings us onto place, or how to get the product out to the consumers, or people who will buy it. Will it be sold only to wholesalers, who then sell it on, or sold directly to shops?

I: Or even <u>directly to individuals, online</u> for example.

T: Yes, that's happening more and more these days.

K: Yes, so then you really need to think about the design of your website ...

I: Yes, that's important. That's connected with promotion, isn't it? The key points there are about <u>communicating with people who might buy the product</u> and encouraging them to buy it.

T: Persuade them to buy it!

K: Ideally, yes.

T: OK, I think we have the key points now.

3 Put students into pairs or small groups and ask them to think of a well-known product. They should discuss the questions given as a preparation for the next stage.

4 Students then use the information to prepare and give a short presentation on the product. Encourage them to use the four Ps as a heading for each section of their presentation. If possible, students could also prepare some visual aids, giving their presentations in a subsequent lesson.

Study skills   page 137

Understanding verbs in essay titles

Aim

This section introduces verbs that are commonly used in academic essay titles at university, as well as in academic reading texts. Although these words are not necessarily used in the IELTS Writing exam, a clear understanding of the difference between them will be helpful to students in their future studies.

1 Many of these words are similar and students may be confused as to their meanings. Ask them to look at the examples and answer the questions. Encourage the use of a learner's dictionary.

Answers

1 *compare* – consider the ways in which things are similar (and possibly different)
  contrast – consider the ways in which things are different (only)
  explain – to tell someone something in a way that helps them understand it better
2 *evaluate* – to give your judgement on the value or worth of something
  describe – to give an account of what something is like (without giving an opinion)
3 *identify* – to say exactly what something is, or to explain a term
  discuss – to write about a subject in detail
4 You *justify* your opinion by giving supporting evidence or reasons for it.

2 Students look at the essay extracts and choose which is an example of each essay question type. Point out to students the kind of language that may be associated with each type of writing, eg linkers such as *but*, are used to compare and contrast. *On balance*, is used to indicate that both sides of an argument have been considered and an opinion is being offered, etc.

Answers

1 justifying an opinion	3 comparing and contrasting
2 evaluating	4 describing

Collocations

Aim

It is useful for students to see that although the meanings are similar the adjectives in this section cannot be used interchangeably because they do not always collocate. The best approach is probably for students to learn a variety of useful collocating adjective noun pairs from this selection.

3 Using a good dictionary, ideally a collocations dictionary, students choose the best adjective in each case. Encourage them to make a record of the correct collocations.

Answers

1 major	5 valuable
2 significant	6 significant
3 fundamental	7 an important
4 an important	

Content overview

Themes

The final unit in this book focuses on different types of success and achievement and provides exam practice in all four IELTS skills areas. It also reviews some of the language covered in previous units.

Exam related activities

Reading

Yes, No, Not given
Summary completion
Multiple choice

Writing

Task 1	Data relating to the Olympic® Games
	Summarizing information
Task 2	Success
	Giving opinions and examples

Listening

Section 2	Multiple choice
	Sentence completion
Section 3	Note completion
	Table completion

Speaking

Part 1	talking about familiar topics
Part 2	describing a successful situation
Part 3	talking about success

Language development

Collocations relating to success
Talking about ability

Test your knowledge

Speaking parts 2 and 3
Vocabulary and grammar from all 12 units

Study skills

Self evaluation

Reading   pages 138–140

Aim

The final reading in the Student's Book focuses on the topic of exams and may help to dispel some of the beliefs commonly held about exams. Some students may be feeling worried about the exam, and this article might provide some reassurance.

1 Students identify the type of success shown in each picture and how the people might have achieved it. Elicit what type of success the students would most like to achieve in their lives and why and how they plan to do this.

Answers

Sporting: winning a race
Education: graduating from university or high school
Professional: winning an appreciation award, possibly for work

2 Ask students to tick any statements which are true for them. You may need to pre-teach *ruined* and *phoney*.

3 Students then discuss their ideas with a partner before brief feedback.

Suggestion

As this is the final reading practice in the book, it might be a good opportunity to give it as a timed reading (20 minutes) for exam practice. Alternatively, follow the procedure outlined below, by doing each question type separately.

4 Yes, No, Not given

Questions 1–8
Look at the statements first, then ask students to read the text to find if the statements reflect the views of the writer. Remind them that a statement may be logical, but that does not mean that the writer agrees with it, or that it is to be found in the text.

Answers

1 Y (*Some* (careers) *may be closed altogether.*)
2 Y (*The world is teeming with people who have found that to be the case whether they have passed examinations or not.*)
3 N (*Practising what you have to do in the examination room is the key.*)
4 NG
5 Y (*… in comparing yourself with others, you find your performance inadequate … Other people are largely irrelevant. They do not depend for their success upon your lack of success or vice versa.*)
6 N (*They may become more technical, involve more abstract ideas and concepts, involve you in greater specialization and more specialist jargon. This does not mean they become more difficult.*)
7 N (*Examiners do not expect you to have done so.*)
8 NG

Summary completion

Questions 9–12
As students complete the summary, remind them to check that they are using an appropriate part of speech as well as inserting something which makes sense.

Answers
 9 reveal
10 disappointed in
11 ability
12 ineffective

Multiple choice

Question 13
This checks global understanding of the text. Having completed the exercises above students should only need a short time to answer this question.

Answer
C

Listening   pages 140–141

IELTS Listening Section 2: Multiple choice

 Questions 1–5

1 Confirm that this is a talk from someone who is not British, but who studied in Britain. Encourage students to underline key words and phrases. Remind them that they need to listen out for synonyms or similar words to those used in the questions.

Answers

1 C   2 A   3 B   4 B   5 A

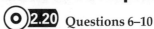

[A = Announcer; AK = Ali Khan]

A: Good afternoon. It's very nice to see so many of you here for our Open Day. I hope that you've enjoyed looking around the campus and have been able to get any questions you have about courses answered. We open this afternoon with a short talk from one of our success stories. Ali Khan is a former student of the university who we are very proud of. He is here this afternoon to tell us a little about his career and how his studies here have helped him. I hope that he will be an inspiration to you.

AK: Thank you very much and good afternoon. It's very nice to be back to visit the university. I have many happy memories of my time here – although I have to admit that the best of these are of social occasions rather than lectures! I first came from Pakistan eleven years ago to study here. I think that the main reason was the reputation that England has. So many English universities have such a strong reputation for academic excellence and a great academic tradition. Also, to be frank, a good British degree is a passport to a higher position and a good job in Pakistan and it has certainly worked that way for me. I'm quite sure I wouldn't have done so well if I hadn't studied here. I originally came to the UK wanting to study Economics and did so here for the first year, but then I found that actually I was much more interested in Politics. I never wanted to become a politician. In my country most people think that they are only a step away from criminals, but I was really fascinated by the way that government functions and the effects that this can have on ordinary people. I wish I had realized this earlier, as it cost me a year's study. When you're choosing your field of study, I think that it's very important to balance what you think will make you employable, with what you're interested in. In my case, as my parents were supporting me, the balance also included what they wanted me to do! Luckily, they were very sympathetic!

Sentence completion

 Questions 6–10

Ensure students understand that they should write one, two or three words. Predict possible answers.

Answers
 6 Ministry of Education
 7 studied in English
 8 flexibility
 9 Development Studies
10 Director

When I graduated in Politics, I went back to Pakistan and began looking for work in the public sector. As I said, I had no intention of becoming a politician, but I felt as if I wanted to do something positive to help my country to develop. I applied for work in the Ministry of Education. The competition for jobs like this is fierce but the fact that I had a good degree from a well-regarded British university made a huge difference. Partly this was because of the standard of education, but I think that there were other reasons why employers favour graduates who have studied overseas. Language, of course, is a major one. Even in Pakistan, where all educated people speak English and the standard is generally high, if an employer knows that you've studied in English to tertiary level, it gives them confidence in your abilities. It's not only language, though. To have had the experience of studying overseas gives you a lot of independence and flexibility. You definitely need to be flexible in order to cope with all of the cultural differences of a different country. Employers value that, I think.

So, I got the job I wanted and worked for six years in the Education sector, before coming back to England to get a Masters degree in Development Studies. I was actually sponsored to do this by the Ministry, and when I finished, last year, I went back to take up a new position of Director of a project to improve technical education in one region of the country. It's an important post and a very interesting one. I suppose that it would be too strong to say that I owe it all to this university, but the education I received here has certainly been a major factor in my success.

2 This exercise focuses on words that are both nouns and verbs. Elicit whether the two examples from the listening show *graduate* as a noun or a verb.

Answers

graduated: verb
graduates: noun
Students look at the four extracts from the listening and choose a suitable word from the box to complete the sentence. They then decide whether it is a noun or a verb. They can check their answers by looking at the audioscripts on pages 174–175.

Answers

1	talk: noun	3	balance: verb
2	visit: verb	4	value: noun

Writing   page 142

IELTS Writing Task 1: Summarizing information

Aim
This section gives an opportunity for students to review and practise the skills necessary to describe data effectively in a typical IELTS Writing Part 1 question.

1 Before looking at the data ask the class to look at the picture (which shows the Olympic® flag being carried at an opening ceremony) and work in pairs to discuss the questions about the Olympic Games.

2 Give students a short time to read the rubric and look at the diagram before discussing the questions in pairs. This will enable them to understand the question and identify the key features and trends shown. This will be useful preparation before they start writing.

Answers

1 generally (but not consistently) upward across the 20-year period
2 China, Great Britain
3 USA, Japan
4 China from 2004 (63) to 2008 (100); Japan from 2000 (18) to 2004 (37)

3 You could do this as a timed writing in class or set as homework.

Answer

See model answer on page 164 of the Student's Book.

Vocabulary   page 143

Suggestion
Students could refer to the *Macmillan Collocations Dictionary* to do these exercises.

1 Students match the nouns in the box with the verbs to form collocations on the theme of success.

Answers

1 to enter a competition, an exam, a race
2 to win a competition, a medal, a prize, a race
3 to pass an exam
4 to gain a qualification
5 to achieve a goal, success

2 Students match the nouns in the box with the adjectives to form collocations.

Answers

1 practical: exam
2 professional: qualification, exam, success
3 sporting: achievement, competition, success
4 great: achievement, success
5 academic: achievement, exam, qualification, success

3 Students use the collocations from exercises 1 and 2 in context by completing the questions. They then ask and answer the questions in pairs. Encourage them to add extra information to their answers.

Answers

1 professional, academic
2 competition, prize, medal, race
3 goals, success
4 achievement, success

Refer students to the Grammar and vocabulary bank on page 159, where there is further practice of collocations with *exam*.

Aim

In this section, students practise the three parts of a typical IELTS Speaking test.

IELTS Speaking Part 1

1 You will need dice for this task (one for each pair or group of students). Students write down questions on the topics given. They then take turns to roll the dice and answer a question for that topic and then give comments on performance. Encourage them to give full answers. Emphasize that this section is on familiar topics and therefore should help the candidate relax. For most students this is the easiest section so it gives them the opportunity to start well. See Unit 1 for more practice of this section of the exam.

Possible answers

1 Where do you come from? Where do you live? What's your home town/city like?
2 What do your parents do? Do you have a big or small family? Do you live with your family?
3 How do you spend your free time? What are your interests? What do you like doing at weekends?
4 Do you work or study? What course are you doing?
5 How often do you go on holiday? Where do you like going on holiday? Which countries have you visited?
6 What are your plans for the future? What are you going to do after this course finishes?

IELTS Speaking Part 2

2 Students read the card and then listen to a student doing the task. Ask them to note down any of the collocations from the Vocabulary section on page 143.

Answers

enter a competition; win (first) prize; win a medal; achieve (your) goals

⊚ 2.21

I'm going to talk about <u>a competition which I entered</u> quite a few years ago when I was 14 or 15. I was never good at sports or music and <u>I couldn't dance or sing</u>, but I had a good imagination so I was very excited when my teacher told us about a national writing competition. I remember we had six weeks to write either a short story or a poem about any subject. I wanted to write a story but I had real difficulty thinking of a good idea and it was only on the day before we had to hand it in that <u>I finally managed to come up with one</u>. I was walking home from school and I was thinking about what present to get my mum for her birthday when I had the idea of writing a poem about my mum.

Once I had the idea, it was easy to write and I handed it in on time. I didn't hear anything for weeks but finally I got a letter saying I was in the final 20. I was invited to a special prize-giving ceremony at a hotel with all the other finalists who came from different schools all over the country. It was really exciting and although <u>I didn't win first prize I did win a medal</u> and certificate and <u>I was able to meet one of my favourite writers</u>, who was presenting the prizes. The whole experience made me realize that <u>it is possible to achieve your goals</u> and it gave me more confidence in myself. I still love writing today and <u>I hope I'll be able to use my talent in my future career</u>.

3 Students have one minute to make notes on the topic, then take it in turns to do the task. When they have finished their talk their partner should ask them one of the follow-up questions provided. Finally, they can give each other feedback on performance. After the pairwork activity, if possible, ask one person to demonstrate with whole-class feedback.

IELTS Speaking Part 3

4 In pairs, students take it in turns to ask and answer the questions. Encourage them to use some of the Useful language in the box to help them begin their answers.

5 Students comment on their partner's responses. After the pairwork activity, if possible, demonstrate with one student and give whole-class feedback.

Language focus   page 145

Talking about ability

1 The four sentence extracts are taken from the previous listening on page 144 (see audioscript ⊚ 2.21). Students read these and then answer questions 1–4 to clarify the meaning and use of the four different structures.

Answers

1 a   2 d   3 b, c   4 b

2 This focuses on checking the form of the structures.

Answers

1 b, c, d
2 a

3 This provides controlled practice of the verb forms. Students have to choose the correct form from the two alternatives provided.

Answers

1 to be able to	4 Were you able to
2 could	5 be able to
3 managed to	

4 This gives freer, more personalized practice of the structures. Students work individually to make notes. Give suggestions as necessary.

5 Students share ideas with a partner. Monitor and check they are correctly using the structures.

Writing   page 145

IELTS Writing Task 2: Giving opinions and examples

Aim
This section gives students an opportunity to review and practise the skills necessary to answer a typical IELTS Writing Task 2 question effectively.

1 Students read the sample task based on the main theme of this unit and underline the key words.

Answers

key words: people, judge, success, money, material possessions, achieved, measured, other ways

2 Discussing the questions in pairs will enable students to understand the task and generate ideas before they start writing. They could also make notes and an outline plan at this stage.

3 This could be a timed task in class, or set as homework.

Answer

See model answer on pages 164–165 of the Student's Book.

Test your knowledge ...   pages 146–147

Aim
This game aims to review some of the language and skills covered in all 12 units in a fun way.

Put students into groups of three or four and provide them with a dice. They will need a counter (button, coin, etc.) to move around the board. Explain that there are four types of question: Speaking Part 2 (pink), Vocabulary (blue), Speaking Part 3 (yellow) and Grammar (green). The numbers in brackets refer to the unit where this topic/language point was covered. Students take it in turns to roll the dice and move their counter. They should do the task or answer the questions on the square they land on. For a Speaking Part 2 (pink) square the other students should time them (a minimum of one minute) and then ask a follow-up question. If students perform the

task satisfactorily or answer the questions correctly, they stay on the same square ready for their next turn. If they get the answer wrong or do not do the task satisfactorily, they must go back two squares and await their next turn. If students need to check their answers they can refer back to the relevant unit. The winner is the first student to reach the red Finish square.

Listening   page 148

IELTS Listening Section 3

Aim
This final Listening not only gives students practice in doing a Section 3 task, but also provides useful advice and tips for IELTS.

Before doing the task, elicit the main difficulties students have with the four IELTS papers. Don't go into too much detail here as some of their ideas may come up in the following exercises.

Note completion

Questions 1–5

(O) **2.22** Students read the instructions and look at the notes about the Listening exam to predict possible answers. Then play the first part of the recording.

Answers

1 the instructions carefully
2 context
3 price
4 an adverb
5 check your spelling

(O) **2.22**

[T =Tutor; E = Eva; P = Pawel]

T: Well, guys, your IELTS test is next week. How are you feeling?

E: Um, to be honest, a bit nervous but quite excited too.

P: Yes, I really want to get on with it now but I have to say it's the listening I'm most worried about. Could you give us some general advice about this part?

T: Yes, of course. Well as you know, there are four parts and they get more difficult as the test goes on but before each section you do have a short time to look at the questions. My first piece of advice is quite simple: <u>read the instructions carefully</u>.

E: Yes, you need to know how many words you can use. I've lost marks on that before.

T: Also, after you've looked at the test paper it should help give you an idea about the kind of situation you're listening to – is it a conversation in a shop or restaurant or a monologue about a particular subject? <u>Make sure you establish the context</u> as this will help activate vocabulary relating to that topic.

E: Good point. And I remember you mentioned the importance of predicting answers to questions, for example, are they looking for a person's name, a place, a date <u>or a price</u>?

T: That's right. It helps to be aware of the kind of information that is being asked for.

E: Didn't you say something about grammar too?

T: Yes. Try and predict what part of speech is coming up.

P: You mean like a noun or verb, <u>or adverb</u> maybe.

T: Exactly. All these strategies should make the actual listening tasks easier.

P: The other thing I keep doing is missing an answer and then losing track of which point I'm at.

T: Right. While you're listening, it's vital to write down answers as quickly as you can but make sure you stay focused on the recording. Try and make a note of possible answers and guess later if you need to.

P: And how much time do we have at the end?

T: You'll get 10 minutes to transfer your answers. <u>Don't forget to check your spelling</u> because you'll lose marks if you make silly mistakes with this. So what's your biggest concern Eva?

Table completion

Questions 6–10

 Students read the instructions and look at the table to predict possible answers. Then play the second part of the recording. This could lead to further discussion on problems students have with the different papers.

Answers

6 poor time management
7 an unknown word
8 leisure
9 grammatical accuracy
10 articles

[T =Tutor; E = Eva; P = Pawel]

T: How are you feeling at the moment?

E: To be honest I'm a bit anxious about all of it, so any advice you could give at this stage would be useful, but it's probably the reading that I find most difficult.

T: Well, I'd say the biggest problem most students have with this is <u>poor time management</u>. They spend too long on the first two passages then run out of time. I would suggest doing some more practice papers giving the same amount of time to each text and make sure you attempt all the answers in the hour.

P: Yes me too, I find some of the passages really hard to understand and I think my main problem is that I don't understand the academic vocabulary.

T: It's probably too late to start learning new words at this stage so it's all about working out the meaning from context. Make sure you don't stop or get 'blocked' when you <u>meet an unknown word</u> but try to guess what it means.

E: What about speaking? Is there anything I can do to improve these skills?

T: Yes definitely, many students find they don't have enough to say in Parts 2 and 3. Why don't you get together with a friend and practise the whole speaking test – ask and answer questions on familiar subjects for Part 1 and for the other sections that focus on common IELTS topics – you know, health, travel, education, <u>leisure</u>, that sort of thing.

P: OK. We could do that. And writing? Is it too late to do anything?

T: It's never too late. Apart from not knowing enough about the subject which I touched on before, the biggest difficulty students face and often get marked down for is <u>grammatical accuracy</u>.

P: Yeah, I'm usually OK with tenses but <u>not so good at using articles correctly in my writing</u>. I always miss them out – probably as we don't have them in my language.

T: What you could do is find some writing you've done recently and look at the type of errors you made and the teacher's corrections.

P: Good idea.

T: OK. So you've got plenty of things to work on before your test so you'd better get started! Hope it goes well for both of you.

E: Thanks for all the tips.

P: Yes, it's been useful advice.

Study skills   page 149

Self-evaluation

Aim

Many students find it difficult to identify effective strategies for independent learning. This task helps them to consider their strengths and areas to work on, as well as strategies for improving their skills.

If students are going to take IELTS in the near future, you could begin by asking them how they are going to prepare for the exam. Then look at the first example together and elicit some specific speaking activities, eg *Discuss something in the news with my host family, Avoid talking in my own language in lessons.* Then ask students to complete the questionnaire individually, or they can work on it with a partner, discussing each point. Students may need considerable guidance completing the final column, and as this is the most important part, it will be useful to focus on specific activities that will help students develop their skills for IELTS.

Grammar and vocabulary bank key

Unit 1 Forming questions

1 Have you been to England?
2 Is Jill living in Hong Kong?
3 When did Peter go to Australia?
4 What does he write?
5 How does she travel to school?

Unit 1 Countable/uncountable nouns

1 Oh, no! Not more *homework*!
  Homework is an uncountable noun.
2 There have been a lot of price *rises* in the last few years.
  A lot of takes a plural noun.
3 Every *piece of advice* I get just makes me more confused. *Advice* is uncountable and so we need to use an expression to say how much advice.
4 I don't have *many dollars/much money* in cash, but I can write you a cheque.
  Dollars is plural and so we use *many*; *money* is an uncountable noun and so we use *much*.
5 Can you bring my *luggage*, please?
  Luggage is an uncountable noun.

Unit 1 Parts of speech: nouns and adjectives

1 different
2 independent
3 comfort
4 significant
5 possibilities

Unit 2 Subject–verb agreement

1 travel
2 cycles
3 travel
4 uses
5 is
6 has

Unit 2 Present simple vs present continuous

1
1 a statement of fact
  b temporary situation at the time of speaking
2 a habit – he always lives there
  b temporary situation
3 a routine – this happens every day
  b temporary situation for this week only
4 a statement of fact
  b action in progress when something else happened

2
1 correct
2 He knows Toronto very well.
3 Come on. We are waiting for you.
4 I agree with you.
5 I have a big house.

Unit 2 Collocations

traffic accident
air traffic
heavy traffic
traffic fumes
traffic jams
traffic lights
busy road
main road
road rage
road safety
road users
road works

Unit 3 Articles

1 a
2 The
3 the
4 the
5 the
6 a/an
7 The
8 the
9 the
10 the
11 the

12 the
13 the
14 a
15 a
16 a
17 an
18 the
19 the
20 the

Unit 3 Synonyms

1
1 expedition
2 drive
3 flight
4 voyage
5 outing
6 tour

2
1 flight
2 crossing
3 an expedition
4 tour
5 drive
6 voyage

Unit 3 Collocations

Possible answers
1 frequent/business
2 adventurous/experienced
3 extensively/regularly
4 independently/overseas

Unit 4 Defining relative clauses

1 where
2 that/which/none needed
3 that/which/none needed
4 whose
5 who

Unit 4 Present perfect vs past simple

1 haven't been
2 have lived
3 graduated
4 studied (and I am no longer there)/have studied (and am still studying)
5 have made
6 went
7 has lived (and still does)/lived (but no longer does)

Unit 4 Collocations

1 crime prevention
2 turn to crime
3 crime wave
4 organized crime
5 crime rate
6 petty crime; serious crime/organized crime
7 to solve a crime

Unit 5 Future forms

1 taking (*going to take* is also possible if the speaker is expressing an intention rather than a firm plan)
2 going to fail
3 will probably increase
4 I'll do
5 I'll try (*I'm trying* is also possible if the speaker is responding to a query while running to class)
6 starts

Unit 5 Comparatives and superlatives

Adjective	Comparative	Superlative
rich	*richer (than)*	*the richest*
cold	*colder*	*the coldest*
late	*later (than)*	*the latest*
safe	*safer*	*the safest*
hot	*hotter (than)*	*the hottest*
fit	*fitter*	*the fittest*
dirty	*dirtier (than)*	*the dirtiest*
easy	*easier (than)*	*the easiest*
difficult	*more difficult (than)*	*the most difficult*
intelligent	*more intelligent (than)*	*the most intelligent*
good	*better (than)*	*the best*
bad	*worse (than)*	*the worst*

Unit 5 Work vocabulary

1 was made redundant
2 resigned
3 retrain
4 applying for
5 was offered a job
6 been promoted
7 retire

Unit 6 Non-defining relative clauses

1 Tourists, who mainly visit Bangkok and the islands, are vital to the Thai economy.
2 FairTrade products, which are often more expensive, are increasing in popularity in the West.
3 The president of the charity, who has been in office for seven years, has resigned.
4 The internet, which is widely available in most parts of the world, has made communication much quicker.

Unit 6 The passive

1 are sorted
2 is roasted
3 are loaded
4 are mashed
5 are added
6 is called
7 is heated
8 is blended
9 is tempered
10 is allowed

Unit 6 Verb + noun collocations

1 make
2 do
3 reached
4 go
5 cut
6 take
7 earn
8 put

Unit 7 Phrasal verbs

1 fill it in
2 pick them up
3 switch them off
4 wake him up
5 work it out

Unit 7 Dependent prepositions

1 from
2 on
3 into
4 by
5 in

Unit 7 Synonyms

1
1 manufacture
2 create, invent
3 develop
4 design

2
1 was invented
2 manufactures
3 was designed
4 develop
5 created

Unit 7 Collocations: *make* and *do*

1

Make	Do
a choice	a course
a decision	a degree
a list	an exercise
a loss	an experiment
a mistake	housework
a speech	research
an appointment	some work
money	
progress	

2
1 making
2 do
3 make
4 do; make
5 make

Unit 8 Conditionals

1 will suffer (real)
2 would be able (unreal)
3 is done (real)
4 sweat (real)
5 were (unreal)
6 have (real)

Unit 8 Dependent prepositions

1 to
2 from
3 for
4 with
5 for
6 by
7 in

Unit 8 Collocations

1 symptoms
2 to relieve
3 an illness/a condition
4 prescribed

Unit 9 *-ing* form and infinitive

1 helping
2 learning
3 doing
4 to take
5 studying
6 to lock

Unit 9 Word formation

1 educational
2 qualified
3 knowledge
4 ability
5 memorize
6 intelligence

Unit 10 Expressing preferences

1 to go
2 not go
3 wearing
4 to come
5 didn't smoke

Unit 10 Expressions with future meaning

1 I aim to finish my studies in a year.
2 I might eventually do a PhD.
3 I will soon start my new course.
4 I am likely to work in my father's company eventually.
5 I hope to improve my English gradually.
6 I anticipate staying here at least three years.

Unit 10 Synonyms

1 increasing amounts/more and more
2 indicates/suggests
3 effect/impact
4 consider/discuss
5 situation/state of affairs

Unit 11 Modals of obligation and prohibition: past and present

1 People had to be treated equally regardless of gender.
2 You didn't need to hand in your essay until after the summer.
3 You didn't have to book your train seat in advance.
4 You had to arrive at least an hour before your flight.
5 Higher taxes shouldn't have been imposed on those with lower incomes.
6 People ought not to have thrown litter on the street.

Unit 11 Phrasal verbs

1
aim at: intend
come up with: create
get away with: succeed in not being punished
get on with: continue
kick off: start
look into: investigate

2
1 aimed at
2 kick off
3 look into
4 get away with
5 come up with

Unit 12 Umbrella nouns

1 questions
2 situation
3 problems
4 trend
5 subject

Unit 12 Collocations

Three similar words: do, sit
Two opposite words: fail, pass
Two things an examiner does: mark, set
Three different types of exam: final, oral, practical
Two phrases where *exam* is used as an adjective: nerves, paper

Teacher's notes for photocopiable activities

1 Studying overseas

Exchanging personal information

This activity practises skills for both Speaking Part 1 and Listening section 1 of the IELTS exam.

Preparation

Copy and cut up the cards so there is one for each student in the class. If you have more than 10 students in your class, some of the cards can be duplicated or students can work in pairs. For classes of fewer than 10 students, give stronger students more than one card. You will also need to photocopy a task sheet for each student.

Procedure

1 Distribute cards and tell students the card contains information about their identity. Give them time to read the information.

2 Elicit the question to the first point, ie *What's your name?* Then ask students to prepare questions for the other points on the card. Check in open class that the questions are appropriate and accurate.

3 Tell students that they have to complete the task sheet by asking other students for the missing information. For this task they will need to stand up, move around the classroom and speak to all the other students. Tell them to avoid looking at each other's cards but to ask for repetition and to check spelling and numbers very carefully.

4 Monitor as the students do the task and make a note of common errors.

5 Have a feedback and error correction slot at the end of the activity.

2 Earth today

The environment

This activity develops vocabulary for talking about the environment and practises reading and speaking skills.

Procedure

1 Check students understand the four headings, then ask them to work in pairs or groups and decide which vocabulary should go under which heading.

Possible answers

(Those in brackets are not in the relevant text, but could be linked to the topic)
1 Overfishing: trawl, shoals, part of their staple diet, extinction, ecosystem
2 The Amazon rainforest: logging, livestock, agriculture, wildlife, rainfall (carbon dioxide, ecosystem)
3 Loss of polar sea ice: reflecting sunlight, ice free, melting
4 Ocean dead zones: fertilizers, sewage, vehicle emissions, carbon dioxide, rainfall, pollution (ecosystem)

2 Put the students into groups of four. Each one should read a different text, summarize the main points and then tell the other students in their group about the text they read.

3 Finally students work together to try to put the problems in order of importance. This should give them the opportunity to use the vocabulary from the first stage.

3 All around the world

Expressing figures

This activity practises skills for Listening section 1 and Speaking Part 1 of the IELTS exam. It also gives students the opportunity to complete a Speaking Part 2 task.

Procedure

1 Students match the figures to their descriptions.

Answers

1 e	3 f	5 a	7 d	9 h
2 i	4 g	6 j	8 b	10 c

2 Students work in pairs to discuss the correct pronunciation of the figures. Use feedback to help with any difficulties.

3 Students match the questions with the responses.

Answers

1 f	3 i	5 d	7 c	9 h
2 g	4 j	6 e	8 b	10 a

4 Students ask and answer the questions and write their partner's responses in the final column.

5 Students choose one of the topics and spend one minute preparing their answer, making notes. They then work in pairs to do the task, giving their partner feedback on their performance.

4 Crime and punishment

Punishment at school

This activity extends some of the topics covered in Unit 4 and introduces new vocabulary related to school punishment. It practises skills for Speaking Part 3 of the IELTS exam.

Procedure

1 Lead in with a general discussion about school punishment.

2 Students match the punishments with definitions.

Answers

1 b	2 d	3 f	4 e	5 c	6 a

3 Students work in groups of three or four to discuss the situations and decide on a suitable punishment. Encourage them to use the language to give opinions, agree and disagree.

4 Students should come to an agreement about the seriousness of the situations by putting them in order.

5 A career or a job?

Find out about …

This integrated skills activity gives students practice in carrying out a small scale research task and writing up the findings. This will give them the opportunity to use some of the language from this and previous units, which is relevant for IELTS Writing task 1.

Preparation

Copy one card for each group of three or four students. For larger classes you can duplicate the cards. You

will also need some large paper/card or a flip chart on which students can present their findings.

Procedure

1 Divide the class into small groups and tell them they are going to conduct a small class survey. Give each group a card and time to look at the information.

2 Students should prepare questions for each point on the card and think of one more question on this topic. Monitor to check that the questions are well-formed.

3 Students carry out the survey amongst their classmates to find out the answers to their questions. They should keep a note of the responses.

4 Once they have collected the information, they should decide the most appropriate way to present the data (bar chart, pie chart, table, etc.) They then draw clear diagrams on the paper provided.

5 Students should write some sentences to describe the key information for each question,
eg *More than half the class …*
The majority of students …
Everybody/nobody …
Approximately 60% of the group …

6 Students present their findings to the rest of the class.

Follow-up

Write an IELTS Task 1 answer about the data collected (150 words minimum).

6 Globalization

A global quiz

This activity practises language covered in this unit (the passive) in the form of a quiz relating to globalization.

Preparation

Copy and cut up the page into the three sections as shown. You will need one copy per pair.

Procedure

1 To lead in to the quiz, students work in pairs to discuss the questions in the first section. Conduct whole class feedback.

2 Divide the class into two groups, A and B, and hand out the appropriate part of the quiz. Students should work with someone from the same group to complete the questions using the verbs in the passive. As they do this, monitor to check accuracy.

Answers

Student A
1 has been published / is published
2 was won
3 is visited
4 was introduced
5 is eaten
6 is found

Student B
1 is understood
2 was watched
3 was visited
4 was first worn
5 is eaten
6 has been sold

1 Regroup the students so that there is at least one A and one B in each group. This could be done in pairs, small groups or even as a whole class activity. Students take it in turns to ask and answer the questions (the answers are provided in brackets). The winning team is the one with the most correct answers.

Follow-up

Students research another global product/food/company, etc. and present their findings to the rest of the class.

7 Gadgets and gizmos

Balloon debate

This activity practises language covered in this unit (describing objects and their purpose) and also gives students the opportunity to hold a group discussion in the form of a balloon debate.

Preparation

Copy one worksheet for every student in the class.

Procedure

1 Students match the pictures to the words, using dictionaries to check answers.

2 In pairs, students take it in turns to describe an item for their partner to guess.

3 Balloon debate: students work individually to choose the five inventions (from the 20) which they think are

the most useful in everyday life. Encourage them to make notes of the reasons for their choices.

4 In pairs, students compare their choices. As a pair, they must reach a consensus to agree on the five most useful inventions so should give opinions and reasons to try to persuade their partner to agree with their view.

5 Put each pair with another pair and repeat the process in stage 4 until they reach agreement within a specified time limit. You may want to repeat this stage with groups of eight before moving to the final whole class discussion.

6 Finally, bring the whole class together to decide on the five most useful inventions.

8 Health and medicine

Topics for discussion

This activity practises and reviews common collocations from Units 1 to 8 and uses these as a focus for discussion.

Preparation

Copy one worksheet for each group of three or four students.

Procedure

1 Students work in pairs to match the words to form common collocations. All of these can be found in Units 1 to 8.

Answers

Tourist attractions
Higher education
Successful career
Road safety
Global trade
Crime rate
Social networking
Balanced diet

2 Students complete the statements with one of the collocations.

Answers

1 Global trade	5 road safety
2 successful career	6 social networking
3 Higher education	7 tourist attractions
4 balanced diet	8 crime rate

3 Students work in groups of three or four and discuss the statements, saying whether they agree or disagree and giving reasons and examples.

4 As a follow-up, students can choose one of the topics and produce a Writing Task 2 answer.

9 All in the mind

Education

This activity develops students' awareness of which verbs to use with *-ing* and infinitive and practises skills for the IELTS Speaking Test Parts 1 and 2.

Procedure

1 Students look at the statements and decide if the verbs should be *-ing* or infinitive.

Answers

1 Think about your first English lesson, or first lesson with this teacher. What can you remember doing?
2 Why did you decide to learn English?
3 Have you ever tried to learn another language (apart from English)? Was it difficult? Did you succeed?
4 What do you like doing best? Speaking or grammar? Why?
5 Have you ever tried listening to the radio to improve your English? Do you think it's a good idea?
6 How often do you remember to do your homework? What helps you to remember?
7 Do you ever try to avoid using a particular grammar point because it's too difficult? If so, which one(s)?
8 Is there anything you regret (not) doing when you were at school?
9 What do you consider to be the most important school subjects? Why?
10 What opportunities do you have to practise speaking English?
11 What do you want to do with your IELTS qualification when you have it?
12 What IELTS score do you hope to get?

2 Students work in pairs to ask and answer the questions from exercise 1. This is similar to the kind of questions they may be asked in Part 1 of the Speaking Test. Encourage them to add examples and details.

3 Students then take it in turns to carry out the instructions on the Part 2 Speaking cards. Monitor and note any difficulties for group feedback.

10 Leisure time

Shopping 'is good for your health'

This activity develops reading skills (skimming and scanning), using an authentic text and then goes on to encourage students to notice and use useful vocabulary related to the topics of health and shopping. Students carry out a survey and write up a report.

Procedure

1 Draw students' attention to the title of the text and encourage prediction.

2 Students then skim the text to check their predictions. At this stage you could briefly ask students if the facts in the text surprised them, if they spend time shopping or exercising, etc.

3 Students then read the text again, this time scanning it to find the relevance of the numbers given.

Answers

385 – How many calories the average British woman burns shopping.
150 – How far (in miles) the average British woman walks every year while shopping.
10 – How many shoppers were tested.
2,000 – How many female shoppers were surveyed.
2.5 – How many hours women spend on average browsing in shops per week.
50 – How many minutes men typically spend shopping per week.
1.5 – How far (in miles) men typically walk while shopping each week.
63 – The percentage surveyed who did not regard shopping as adequate exercise.
7,300 – The number of steps women take on average while shopping.
10,000 – The number of steps recommended by the NHS.

4 Ask students to underline words and phrases related to shopping or exercise.

Possible answers:

Shopping
a trip to the shops
bargains
die-hard shoppers
shoppers
while away the hours browsing
Health/exercise
pedometers
calories
consider/calculate the health benefits of an activity
adequate exercise
workout

5 Students use the table to conduct a class survey. Conduct a brief feedback, pulling out the main points, such as any differences between men and women in the class.

6 Finally, students use the language given to write up their findings in a short report.

11 The art of advertising

Conducting a survey and report

This activity gives students practice in discussing and negotiating and in giving a small presentation. It also recycles the advertising-related vocabulary from the text.

Preparation

You will need some large paper/card or a flip chart on which students can make their posters.

Procedure

1 Divide the class into small groups and tell them they will work together in teams of three or four to design, develop and launch a brand new chocolate bar. They will present their ideas to the class and vote on the product most likely to be successful.

2 Ask students to look at the questions and underline the vocabulary related to the topic of advertising.

Answers

target market, product, key features, packaged, promote, word of mouth, billboards, TV commercials, stealth marketing, guerrilla marketing

3 Next ask students to use the questions to help them prepare a short presentation about their product.

4 Groups of students then take it in turn to make their presentations. The other groups have to carry out the tasks given while they are listening.

5 Finally the groups vote on the best product and give each other feedback on the presentations.

12 Success and achievement

IELTS quiz

This activity tests students' overall knowledge of the IELTS exam and gives them the opportunity to practise both speaking and listening.

Preparation

Copy and cut up a worksheet for each pair of students.

Procedure

1 Divide the class into pairs, A and B, and hand out the relevant copy of the quiz. Tell students not to look at their partner's paper. Students then test each other's knowledge of the IELTS exam by taking it in turns to ask their questions. To make this more competitive you could do this in larger groups and award points for correct answers.

2 As a follow-up, ask students to write five more questions for the other team, or write five pieces of advice for a student new to the IELTS exam.

1 Studying overseas

Exchanging personal information

Name: Jeff Bremner Nationality: Canadian Age: 21 Work/Study: Studying Chemistry Contact number: 0683 472001 Interests: skiing, listening to rap music	Name: Katarina Deyna Nationality: Polish Age: 27 Work/Study: Police officer Contact number: 0792 341885 Interests: dancing, playing the violin
Name: Mohammed Omeri Nationality: Egyptian Age: 18 Work/Study: Studying Engineering Contact number: 0234 661587 Interests: horse riding, snooker	Name: Faisa Yakub Nationality: Malaysian Age: 20 Work/Study: Studying Medicine Contact number: 0331 689227 Interests: swimming, reading poetry
Name: Abdulla Khan Nationality: Pakistani Age: 30 Work/Study: Businessman Contact number: 0417 652833 Interests: cooking, cycling	Name: Christiana Falcao Nationality: Brazilian Age: 23 Work/Study: Nurse Contact number: 0246 443912 Interests: basketball, playing the guitar
Name: Mario Rossi Nationality: Italian Age: 17 Work/Study: Studying Biology Contact number: 0543 871192 Interests: football, listening to rock music	Name: Gina Thomson Nationality: Australian Age: 22 Work/Study: Fitness instructor Contact number: 0796 551342 Interests: squash, scuba diving
Name: Orhan Shakan Nationality: Turkish Age: 33 Work/Study: Accountant Contact number: 0841 769935 Interests: chess, running	Name: Stephanie Muller Nationality: German Age: 19 Work/Study: Studying Law Contact number: 0942 883174 Interests: computer games, painting

Task Sheet

Name	Nationality	Age	Work/Study	Contact number	Interests
Jeff Bremner					
			Police officer		
	Egyptian				
				0331 689227	
		30			
Christiana Falcao					
			Studying Biology		
	Australian				
				0841 769935	
		19			

111

2 Earth today

1 You are going to read four texts about the environment. Which items of vocabulary in the box do you think came from which text?

1 Overfishing   2 The Amazon rainforest   3 Loss of polar sea ice   4 Ocean dead zones

> trawl   logging   livestock   agriculture   wildlife   rainfall   shoals   reflecting sunlight   ice free
> fertilizers   sewage   melting   vehicle emissions   carbon dioxide   part of their staple diet
> extinction   ecosystem   pollution   drought

2 Work in groups of four. Read one text each (1 to 4) and check your predictions.

Four major environmental problems

1 Overfishing

Fish is a great source of protein. It doesn't require farming and it's healthy. As such, for millions of people worldwide it's a staple part of their diet. As a result, fishing is big business. Huge ships trawl the oceans, using sonar to track and catch shoals of fish. It is estimated
that over 90% of large fish such as cod and tuna have already been caught. Many species are on the verge of extinction. We are fast heading towards a global collapse of all species currently fished – possibly even by 2048. This would obviously have a major impact on the whole ecosystem.

2 The Amazon rainforest

People have known about the threat to the Amazon rainforest for a long time, but it is still under serious attack. Recent research suggests that agriculture, fire, logging, drought and livestock will significantly damage over 50% of the rainforest over the next two decades and may destroy as much as 80% of the wildlife living there.

This isn't just a problem for the Amazon area. Losing this much of the rainforest will accelerate global warming and could affect rainfall in other parts of the world. The study says that the 'point of no return', from which recovery will be impossible, is no more than 20 years away.

3 Loss of polar sea ice

Polar sea ice is melting at a level never seen before. Records started in 1972, but scientists are saying that the ice is now at a lower level than it has been for at least 8000 years. It is estimated that within the next 40 years the Arctic may be largely ice free during the summer months.

This may not sound devastating, but Arctic ice plays a vital role in regulating the climate on Earth by reflecting sunlight and keeping the polar region cool. The loss of polar sea ice is both a consequence of global warming and a contributing factor.

4 Ocean dead zones

It may sound like something from a horror film, but the ocean dead zones are only too real. In oceans around the world, these are areas where almost nothing can live because there is no oxygen. This is caused by excess nitrogen from fertilizers, vehicle emissions and sewage.

The number of dead zones is increasing fast. Since the 1960s their number has doubled every 10 years. Their area can be as much as 45,000 square miles. Global warming is likely to exacerbate the problem as a rise in carbon dioxide causes increased rainfall and more pollution to run from rivers to the sea.

3 Tell the other people in your group about the text you read. What are the key points made? What facts did you find particularly shocking or memorable?

4 Try to put the problems into order of importance. Give reasons for your decisions.

3 All around the world

Expressing figures

1 Match the figures 1 to 10 with their descriptions a to j.

1 45kph	a a temperature
2 5 Vicarage Gardens	b a time
3 brandy123@gmail.co.uk	c a date
4 0121 74839921	d a measurement
5 32°C	e a speed
6 €17	f an email address
7 57cm	g a telephone number
8 8.25am	h a decade
9 1960s	i an address
10 05/09/2002	j a price

2 Work with a partner. How do you say each of the figures?

3 Now match the questions 1 to 10 to the answers a to j.

1 What's the average summertime temperature in your home town?	a 70 miles per hour.	
2 What's your mobile number?	b Thirty-five pounds.	
3 What decade were you born in?	c About one metre seventy.	
4 What's your email address?	d 29 High Street, Swindon.	
5 What's your address?	e The 4th of November.	
6 When's your birthday?	f About 20 degrees, I think.	
7 How tall are you?	g It's 0 double 7 4 4 6 2 4 8 5.	
8 How much did your shoes cost?	h At half past ten.	
9 What time did you go to bed last night?	i The 1970s.	
10 What's the speed limit on motorways in your country?	j J mills – that's J-M-I-double L-S seventy two at hotmail dot com.	

4 Ask your partner the same questions and make a note of his/her answers in the third column.

5 Choose one of the Speaking Part 2 tasks below. Spend one minute planning your talk. Try to speak for at least one minute on the topic.

Talk about a date which is significant in your life. You should say – what the date is – what happened on that date – how this date makes you feel and explain why the date is so important to you.
Talk about a date which is significant for your country. You should say – what the date is – what happens/happened on that date – how this date makes you feel and explain why the date is so important for your country.

4 Crime and punishment

Punishment at school

1 Discuss these questions with your partner:

What kind of things would you consider bad behaviour at school?

What punishments were used in your school for bad behaviour?

2 Match the names of different kinds of punishments with their definitions.

1 a warning	a being forced to leave school permanently because of bad behaviour
2 corporal punishment	b telling someone they will be punished if they do something bad again.
3 suspension	c writing a sentence such as I will not eat in class many times
4 detention	d physical punishment, eg hitting someone
5 writing lines	e staying at school when the other children have gone home
6 expulsion	f removing someone from school for a short time

Can you think of any other punishments that are used in schools?

3 In groups discuss these situations. What kind of punishment do you think they deserve and why?

a Two fifteen-year-old boys have been caught smoking on school premises.

b Two thirteen-year-old girls were found in the town centre during school hours.

c A sixteen-year-old girl has been accused of cyber-bullying another girl on a social-networking site. The victim is so upset she has been absent from school.

d A fourteen-year-old boy swore at a female teacher after he was told to stop talking during a lesson.

e A twelve-year-old has persistently arrived between fifteen and twenty minutes late every morning for a week.

f A fourteen-year-old boy has been caught writing on the back of a toilet door with a marker pen. The door will need to be repainted.

g In an exam, two fifteen-year-old girls are discovered to be cheating by using their mobile phones.

h A boy has come to school wearing jeans instead of the school uniform. He also has a pierced nose. He has already been warned twice about this.

Giving opinions	Agreeing and disagreeing
I feel/believe that ... *In my opinion ...* *I'm sure that ...* *I tend to think that ...*	*I strongly agree with this view ...* *I disagree with the view that ...* *I do not believe that ...*

4 In small groups, put the situations in order from least to most serious, then agree on a final order as a class.

115

5 A career or a job?

Find out about …

Find out about transport

– How students come to class?
– Travel preference: train or bus?
– How many students have been on a flight of over three hours?
– Weekly expenditure on public transport?
– Bicycle use?
Think of one more question on this topic.

Find out about travel

– How many countries visited?
– Most popular country to visit?
– Type of holiday – beach, city, activity, etc?
– Holiday in own country or abroad?
– Length of time on holiday?
Think of one more question on this topic.

Find out about education

– Area of study: arts, business or science?
– How long spent studying per week?
– Exams or coursework?
– How many are interested in postgraduate study?
– Length of time learning English?
Think of one more question on this topic.

Find out about work

– Number of people with jobs: full- or part-time?
– Most popular sector: business, education, health, retail?
– Company or self-employed?
– Job satisfaction or salary?
– Ideal retirement age for men and women?
Think of one more question on this topic.

6 Globalization

A global quiz

Work in pairs. Can you think of ...

– an overseas product which is available in your country?
– an international food which is popular in your country?
– a book which you have read (in your own language) which was originally written in another language?
– a film you have seen which was made in another language?
– an international shop which has stores in your country?
– a word in your language which comes from another language?

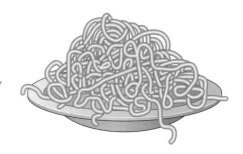

STUDENT A

Complete the questions by choosing a verb from the box and putting it in the correct form of the passive (either present simple, past simple or present perfect).

win	publish	eat	find	introduce	visit

1   Which series of books _____ in more than 65 countries? *(Harry Potter™)*

2   Which worldwide sporting event _____ in 2006 by Italy and in 2010 by Spain? *(the football World Cup)*

3   Which website _____ an estimated one billion times every day? *(YouTube™)*

4   Which number puzzle _____ in Japan in the 1980s? *(sudoku)*

5   Which spicy Asian dish _____ all over the world and is particularly popular in the UK? *(curry)*

6   Which Swedish shop _____ in more than 30 countries worldwide? *(IKEA®)*

Ask Team B your questions.

STUDENT B

Complete the questions by choosing a verb from the box and putting it in the correct form of the passive (either present simple, past simple or present perfect).

visit	watch	sell	understand	eat	wear

1   Which expression _____ all over the world to mean *yes, alright, agreed*? *(OK)*

2   Which 2008 sporting event _____ by an estimated four billon people all over the world? *(the Beijing Olympic® Games opening ceremony)*

3   Which European country _____ by about 76 million foreign tourists in 2010. *(France)*

4   Which popular item of clothing _____ first _____ in California in the 1850s. *(jeans)*

5   Which Japanese food _____ all over the world? *(sushi)*

6   Which TV singing competition _____ to more than 40 countries around the world? *(the Idol™ series)*

Ask Team A your questions.

117

7 Gadgets and gizmos

Balloon debate

1 Match the pictures of everyday items with words from the box. Use your dictionary to check your answers.

2 Take it in turns to describe a picture to your partner, who will guess which item you are talking about. Use the following phrases:
eg *It's used for ... + -ing, It's used in the kitchen ...,*
You use it to ... + infinitive, It's made of ...

rubber   clothes peg   plaster   comb   can opener   bottle opener   sticky tape   pencil sharpener
TV remote control   lipstick   ear plugs   paper clip   calculator   remote car keyfob   toothpick
sticky notepaper   potato peeler   egg box   nailfile   clothes hanger

3 Individually choose the five items (from the 20) that you think are the most useful inventions. Make notes about why you think each item is useful.

_____

_____

_____

_____

4 Persuade other students that your items are the most useful.

8 Health and medicine

Topics for discussion

1 Work in pairs. Match the words to form a common collocation.
(Note all these collocations appear in units 1 to 8.)

1 tourist	a career
2 higher	b trade
3 successful	c networking
4 road	d rate
5 global	e attractions
6 crime	f diet
7 social	g education
8 balanced	h safety

2 Complete the sentences with an appropriate collocation.

1 _____ makes rich countries richer.

2 Having a _____ is one of the most important goals in life.

3 _____ is too expensive and should be free for everyone.

4 A _____ is the best way to stay healthy.

5 Governments should spend more money on improving _____.

6 The drawbacks of online _____ outweigh the benefits.

7 Popular _____ are usually too expensive and crowded to be enjoyable .

8 The most serious problem in urban areas is the rising _____.

3 Discuss these statements giving opinions, examples and reasons for your comments.

4 Choose one of the statements and write an IELTS Task 2 answer.
Don't forget to generate ideas, make an outline plan before you start writing, then check your answer carefully.

9 All in the mind

1 Look at the questions below and choose the correct form.

> **1** Think about your first English lesson, or first lesson with this teacher. What can you remember <u>to do/doing</u>?

> **2** Why did you decide <u>to learn/learning</u> English?

> **3** Have you ever tried <u>to learn/learning</u> another language (apart from English)? Was it difficult? Did you succeed?

> **4** What do you like <u>to do/doing</u> best? Speaking or grammar? Why?

> **5** Have you ever tried <u>to listen/listening</u> to the radio to improve your English? Do you think it's a good idea? Why/why not?

> **6** How often do you remember <u>to do/doing</u> your homework? What helps you to remember?

> **7** Do you ever try to avoid <u>to use/using</u> a particular grammar point because it's too difficult? If so, which one(s)?

> **8** Is there anything you regret (not) <u>to do/doing</u> when you were at school?

> **9** What do you consider <u>to be/being</u> the most important school subjects? Why?

> **10** What opportunities do you have to practise <u>to speak/speaking</u> English?

> **11** What do you want <u>to do/doing</u> with your IELTS qualification when you have it?

> **12** What IELTS score do you hope <u>to get/getting</u>?

2 In pairs, ask and answer the questions from exercise 1. Remember to add some details and examples.

3 Take it in turns to talk about one of the following cards.

> **A** Describe your favourite subject at school.
>
> You should say
> • What your teacher(s) were like.
> • What you remember doing in the class.
> • What you particularly liked about the subject.
> Explain what impact this subject has had on your life.

> **B** Describe something you have learned to do which took a lot of practice.
>
> You should say
> • Why you wanted to do it.
> • When and for how long you practised doing it.
> • Whether you enjoyed practising it or not, and why.
> Explain what impact learning to do it has had on your life.

10 Leisure time

1 Work in pairs. Look at the headline below. In what ways do you think shopping might be good for your health?

Shopping 'is good for your health'

Shopping might not be good for your wallet, but it could be good for your health, new research suggests.

2 Quickly read the text and check your predictions.

Walking between shops and lifting heavy shopping bags provides a workout which burns 385 calories a week for the average British woman, according to the analysis.

The average British woman also walks more than 150 miles a year in search of bargains, the equivalent of walking from London to Hull.

Department store Debenhams tested 10 shoppers (five male and five female) with calorie-counting pedometers, and surveyed 2,000 female shoppers in order to calculate the health benefits of a trip to the shops.

It found that women cover an average of nearly three miles during the 2.5 hours they spend browsing the shops every week.

In contrast, men typically spend just 50 minutes shopping and cover just 1.5 miles.

A spokesman for Debenhams said: 'Our research has shown that Britons love to shop and will happily while away the hours browsing the High Street.

The added health benefits we have discovered mean that exercise and losing weight are easily achievable through everyday activities.'

However, while it might be a handy excuse for die-hard shoppers, the survey found that most people do not consider the

health benefits when deciding to go shopping.

Sixty-three per cent of those surveyed did not regard shopping as adequate exercise, even though the study points out that women take an average of 7,300 steps every trip, close to the NHS recommendation of 10,000 steps per day.

Almost half of women admitted they 'shop till they drop', walking for hours on end without taking a break in order to find what they are looking for.

The spokesman added: 'We encourage our customers to wear pedometers on their next shopping trip to see the results for themselves.'

3 Read the text again. What do the following numbers in the text represent?

385   *How many calories the average British woman burns shopping.*

150   _____

10   _____

2,000   _____

2.5   _____

50   _____

1.5   _____

63   _____

7,300   _____

10,000   _____

4 Underline all the words and phrases you can find in the text which are connected with shopping or health.

5 Carry out a short survey, asking both men and women if possible.

How long do you spend shopping each week?
Do you think that shopping is good exercise?
Do you ever 'shop 'til you drop'?

6 Now write up your findings in a short report. You could use some of the Useful language given below.

We carried out a short survey into shopping and exercise, asking _____ women and _____ men about their shopping habits.   We found that …   In contrast …/However, …   _____% of those surveyed said that …   Most of the men/women said that …   Almost half the class said that …

122

11 The art of advertising

Launching a new chocolate bar

In this task you will work together in teams of three or four to design, develop and launch a brand new chocolate bar. You will present your ideas to the class and vote on the product most likely to be successful.

1 First look at the following questions and underline all the vocabulary related to the topic of marketing.
  1 What is the target market for your product? Think about age, gender, income, etc.
  2 What key features will the product have? Think about ingredients, taste, shape. What will make it different from all the other chocolate bars on the market?
  3 What will you call your product, and why?
  4 How will it be packaged? Make sure your choices are appropriate for your target market.
  5 How much will it cost? Where will it be available to buy?
  6 How will you promote the product? Word of mouth, billboards, TV commercials? Will you use any stealth or guerrilla marketing?

2 Now use the questions above to guide you in preparing your presentation.

3 Design a poster showing your product and add a slogan. You may also make up a jingle if you wish. Then decide which member of your team will present which part of the presentation. Everyone should contribute to the talk.

4 Give a group presentation about your product. While you are listening to the other presentations:
  • Think of an appropriate question to ask the group at the end of each presentation.
  • Make a note of positive aspects of the presentation itself (eg clearly structured, good range of relevant vocabulary used) and any aspects that could be improved.
  • Decide which chocolate bar is likely to be most successful and why. (You are not allowed to vote for your own product).

	Presentation 1	Presentation 2	Presentation 3	Presentation 4
Name of product				
Strong and weak points about product and marketing of product				
Strong and weak points about presentation				

PHOTOCOPIABLE

12 Success and achievement

IELTS quiz

Student A

1 In Part 1 of the Speaking Test will the examiner ask you easy or difficult questions? *(easy – on familiar topics)*

2 Name four possible topics for Speaking Part 2. *(a job you'd like to do, a book you've read, an item of technology you own, film you've seen, etc.)*

3 You have a minute to prepare your answers in Speaking Part 3. True or false? *(false – you have to answer the questions immediately)*

4 How many texts are in the Reading Test? *(three)*

5 In the Reading Test you have time to transfer your answers at the end of the time limit. True or false? *(false – one hour including time to transfer your answers)*

6 Name four question types that you have to answer. *(Multiple choice, True/False/Not Give, Note completion, Paragraph matching)*

7 How much time is recommended for IELTS Writing Task 2? *(40 minutes)*

8 You are expected to give your opinions about the data in the diagrams. True or false? *(false – describe the data but don't give personal views)*

9 Are you allowed to use correction fluid in the writing tasks? *(no)*

10 How many sections are there in the Listening Test? *(four)*

11 Spelling is very important in the Listening Test. True or false? *(true – incorrect spelling will be penalized)*

12 How much time do you have to transfer your answers at the end of the Listening Test? *(10 minutes)*

- ✂

Student B

1 Name five topics the examiner might ask you about in Speaking Part 1. *(hometown/city, family, interests, work/study, future plans)*

2 What is the maximum length of time you can speak for in Speaking Part 2? *(maximum two minutes, minimum one minute)*

3 In Speaking Part 3 the examiner will ask you questions on a range of different topics. True or false? *(false – the one topic will be connected with the Part 2 topic)*

4 How many questions do you have to answer in the Reading Test? *(40)*

5 You must use a pencil in the Reading Test. True or false? *(true – pens are not allowed in this section)*

6 Are dictionaries allowed in the Reading Test? *(no)*

7 What is the minimum number of words expected for Writing Task 1? *(150 minimum)*

8 Writing Task 2 is worth more marks than Writing Task 1. True or false? *(true – Task 2 is weighted more heavily)*

9 What writing style should you use in the writing tasks? *(academic/formal/impersonal)*

10 How many questions do you have to answer in the Listening Test? *(40)*

11 You hear each part of the Listening Test once only. True or false? *(true)*

12 In the Listening Test how much time do you have at the end of each section to check your answers? *(half a minute)*

Macmillan Exams Portal

- Detailed overview of all English language exams
- Exams news
- Author videos
- Student and teacher course material recommendations and more…

Apps for IELTS

This new range of Apps offers an innovative approach to preparing students for the IELTS exams. With a wealth of interactive content written by Sam McCarter, author of bestselling *Ready for IELTS* and the new lower-level *IELTS Introduction*, the apps focus on the skills needed for success at IELTS as well as providing a complete range of exam-type practice exercises.

Key Features
- Covers areas such as reading speed, ability to respond effectively to the examiner and self-correcting in the writing paper
- Students can measure their progress by interacting with 'can do' statements linked to key skills areas

For more information, visit www.macmillaneducationapps.com

www.macmillanexams.com

IELTS ESSENTIALS FROM

IELTS Introduction

Sam McCarter

Taking your first
IELTS steps

▸ 12 units packed with
exercises aimed at
developing listening,
speaking, reading and
writing skills
▸ Essential IELTS task tips
▸ Collocation exercises
▸ Model answers for writing
tasks

IELTS Foundation
Second Edition

Andrew Preshous / Rachael Roberts
Joanna Preshous / Joanne Gakonga

▸ For students aiming for IELTS
band 4-5.5
▸ This course provides a
comprehensive package,
including extra self-study
material that means students
will achieve success with
confidence and ease
▸ The scaffolding of the grammar
allows clear strategies to be
developed as students move
from lower to higher bands
▸ Supported by a Teacher's
Book with sample answers,
photocopiables, full answer
keys and recording scripts
▸ Includes Class Audio CDs

IELTS Graduation

Mark Allen / Debra Powell /
Dickie Dolby

▸ This focused, topic-based book
will train the students in the
skills required to achieve a high
IELTS score
▸ Language Focus, Writing and
Pronunciation sections build up
the students' confidence and
competence in these skills
▸ Strategy and tip boxes offer hints
on how to tackle the various IELTS
tasks
▸ The Student's Book is supported
by the Teacher's Book with full
information on all parts of the exam

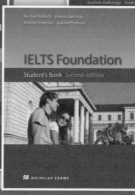

MACMILLAN EXAMS

Ready for IELTS

Sam McCarter

Bestseller

This IELTS preparation course combines the successful elements of the 'Ready for...' series and an experienced author team to ensure students aiming for IELTS bands 5–6.5 are ready for success.

Key Features

▸ Two-page review section at the end of each unit with exam-style tasks

▸ 'Ready for...' sections focus on each IELTS exam paper, giving extra support and tips

▸ Special emphasis on word building, collocations and phrasal verbs, paraphrasing, synonyms and polysemy

▸ Topic-based wordlists

▸ Model answers, graded by an examiner, provide excellent support for writing

Tips for IELTS

Sam McCarter

This slim, definitive little book is packed full of all the information you need to know about the four skills tested in IELTS: hints on how to tackle specific types of questions; strategies on how to avoid common mistakes, and increase speed and accuracy; and useful language to be aware of and to use. This is the sort of book that can be used for quick reference, for revising and for checking progress.

IELTS Language Practice

Michael Vince // Amanda French

An in-depth, detailed approach to English grammar and vocabulary.

A thorough and comprehensive series that ensures students' confidence with language through the progressive levels.

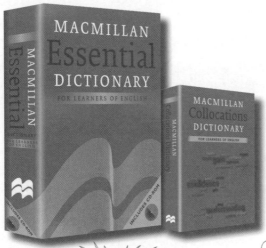